EVALUATION IN PRIMARY EDUCATION

Encyclopaedia of Primary Education Series

EVALUATION IN PRIMARY EDUCATION

Edited by

B.V. Verghese

ANMOL PUBLICATIONS PVT. LTD.

NEW DELHI - 110 002 (INDIA)

ANMOL PUBLICATIONS PVT. LTD.
4374/4B, Ansari Road, Daryaganj
New Delhi - 110 002
www.anmolbooks.com

Evaluation in Primary Education

First Edition, 2002

ISBN 81-261-1050-3

PRINTED IN INDIA

Published by J.L. Kumar for Anmol Publications Pvt. Ltd., New Delhi - 110 002 and Printed at Mehra Offset Press, Delhi.

Contents

Preface

As important as evaluation is to education, and the classroom teacher, the process is not unique to education. People in all walks of life make evaluations constantly whether they realize it or not. Take example of a person crossing the street. He makes an evaluation when he looks both ways, estimates the speed of approaching vehicles, and then decides either to cross or not to cross the street.

Here in this book role of evaluation in primary education is described pros and cons. The authoritative information gathered from different sources is arranged in logical sequence. Topics like Evaluation, evaluation and assessment, education and school-based evaluation, matching evaluation, primary teacher, politics of primary teacher, OD and primary schools, progressive education and evaluation, evaluation of citizenship, improving classroom testing, strategies and tactics in elementary school classroom, etc. are given elaborate treatment.

I am grateful to all the scholars whose writings and fruits of painstaking research are cited or substantially made use of in this book. I am also thankful to all my friends who have assisted me while preparing the manuscript. Last but not the least I am grateful to Mr. J.L. Kumar, Managing Director, Anmol Publications Pvt. Ltd., New Delhi for undertaking the publication of this work.

—**B.V. Verghese**

1
What is Evaluation ?

There is probably no process more central to teaching than *evaluation*, the process that involves the making of decisions. These decisions are based upon pertinent information, which you have gathered either formally or informally, and considered value judgments. The use of the term *evaluation* has at times been questioned, because of the narrow connotations of good and bad which it sometimes brings to mind. However, you should be cautioned at this point that the meaning of the term is broader in scope than merely decisions of bad and good. Evaluation will be used here to include all types of decisions.

As important as evaluation is to education and the classroom teacher, the process is not unique to education. People in all walks of life make evaluations constantly whether they realize it or not. For example, a person crossing the street makes an evaluation when he looks both ways, estimates the speed of approaching vehicles, and then decides either to cross or not to cross the street, A homemaker shopping for the family dinner makes an evaluation when checking all the meat prices before deciding on a particular cut. A person planting a vegetable garden makes evaluations as to what the type of seeds to plant in the garden after checking characteristics of the plants and the growing conditions in the area.

All of these examples have two characteristics in common. One is that there was some type of decision being made; the other is that there was some type of information input before the decision was made. In all three examples, data in the form of measurements were actively gathered and utilized in the making of the decision. The measurements may have been formal or informal, but they were the basis for the evaluation.

Data gathering can occur in two ways in the evaluation process. One is by data input, and the other by data recall. In data input, the individual actively searches the environment for information which is relevant to the decision at hand. For example, in the case of the man crossing the street, data input would occur when the individual checked for cars and noted their approximate speeds. In the gardening example, the individual planting the garden would input data by reading the seed packages and checking the type and consistency of the soil.

Data recall occurs when the individual remembers information which is pertinent to the decision to be made. The woman purchasing meat for the evening meal might recall recent dinner menus and family members' preferences regarding different types of meat. The person crossing the street might try to remember previous similar experiences in crossing that street or information such as the speed limit on that section of road or whether there were any stop lights on that street to slow down the cars.

As previously mentioned, evaluation consists of decision-making based upon information gathered. One other characteristic of the evaluation process should lie mentioned. This involves the influence of values on the evaluations that people make. *Values* are those beliefs which guide a person's life. Patriotism, love, honesty, and truthfulness are all values. Values influence all evaluations, whether the individual making the evaluation is aware of this or not. In the previously cited instances, personal values toward risk-taking when crossing the street and the importance of money and personal health when buying meat could influence the evaluations made

Let's look now at some examples of educational evaluations. For instance, a teacher assigns certain roles in a play according to unique characteristics of the students. In doing this, the teacher might try to match such factors as the type and the difficulty of role with specific students. These assignments would be evaluations for several reasons. First, they are decisions. Second, they arc based on information that the teacher has gathered such as the personalities of the children and the demands of the different roles. Finally these decisions are based on the teacher's belief that self-confidence, ability to speak in public, and ability to memorize are important skills to encourage in students.

Certain types of educational evaluations are readily apparent. Teachers make evaluations constantly about whether Johnny has learned his multiplication tables, knows the letters of the alphabet, or understands the experiment discussed in last Thursday's class. Often the evaluative nature of this process is emphasized by the fact that the teacher actually gives a grade, which is only one type of evaluation. This giving of grades is an evaluation because it is a decision reached by a teacher based upon data (quizzes, test papers, assignments, or participation in class) and certain values (hard work, obedience, the importance of factual knowledge, or creativity). Notice here how informal measurements and values influence teacher evaluations. A teacher valuing hard work, adherence to rules, and perseverance who notices a student reading during times allotted for homework may consciously or unconsciously react unfavourably. Here the values and the informal measurement of merely noticing the student reading interact to affect the teacher's decision. On the other hand, a teacher who values free spiritedness and a curious mind may react in precisely the opposite way when making the identical informal measurement.

Some other types of evaluations made by teachers may not be so apparent. These do not involve a grade as a judgment. A teacher allowing a student to go out to recess even though he hasn't finished his math work would be an example of an evaluation. In making that decision, she gathered information (the student's restlessness and inability to concentrate) as well as recalled information (past instances in which the student acted this way). She then used this information along with values she had toward children and education and decided that it would be best to allow him to go out and run off some of his excess energy.

If you are aware of factors that enter into the evaluation process, such as informal measurement, you can then make better evaluations. If you understand the importance of the information in the evaluation process, you can strive to make sure that the information that you use is accurate. Also, if you are aware of the values that influence your evaluations, your decisions may become more rational. Now that you have studied the process of evaluation, we hope you will be able to apply this knowledge and make better and more sensitive evaluations in your classroom.

EXERCISE 1.1

Read the scenario that follows and decide whether each numbered statement describes an informal measurement (im) a formal measurement (fm), or an evaluation (e) Then compare your answers to the ones found in the feedback section at the end of the chapter

Miss Anthony wanted her kindergarten students to be prepaid for written symbol recognition so that they could pick out the symbol when its sound was made. Therefore, she needed to determine if her kindergarten class needed more work in sound discrimination before they went into recognition of the written symbols : (1)—She decided to pronounce the words *bird, dog, ball,* dad, *man, none nose,* and *milk* to the children individually and ask them to tell her which ones had the same first sound. (2)— She then checked the students to see if they could match the sounds, and she found that 8 of her 20 students matched all four of the pairs of sounds correctly, while the other 12 incorrectly matched one or more of the pairs.

She separated the children into the group of 12 and the group of 8, which she started on written letter recognition activities. (3)— Then, in order to have smaller groups. Miss Anthony divided the group of 12 into those whose first names started with *A* through *M* and those whose names started with *N* through *Z,* which made six students per group. (4)— She decided to practise first letter sounds with both of these groups by presenting pictures of objects and pronouncing the words.

While Miss Anthony worked with the first group of six, she saw Joey poke Mary and pull her hair. (5)— She also noticed Joey glancing at her as he performed his little disruptions. (6)— She recalled that he had been making himself conspicuous in other activities as well. (7)— She then decided that she wouldn't call more attention to Joey by reprimanding him. (8)— She noticed that Mary seemed to be paying little attention to him.

After Miss Anthony completed her week long activity with her two groups of six, she gave the children each a set of 15 pictures and told them to put all of the pictures that started with the sound of "b" in one pile, those that started with "d" in a second pile, those with "m" in a third, and those with "n" in a fourth. (9)— Based on the results, Miss Anthony moved the top eight into symbol recognition but held the bottom four students back for more work.

TEST APPROACHES

Norm-Referenced Tests

When students go to school, they are assigned to specific classes. This assignment may be very deliberate, based upon subject matter, ability, or age, or it may be random. The point is that students are placed in groups and are therefore measured and evaluated in a group setting. Because the students are in groups and are frequently competing against one another, *norm-referenced* tests have been very popular since World War I. In essence, this approach compares the score of one student to the scores of all the other students in the group. The population or group could be as small as a self-contained classroom or as large is a nationwide sample taking a standardized examination at one given time. When comparing scores, a student's standing within the group is clearly identified. The basic point to remember here is that norm-referenced tests are solely concerned with how one student compares with others.

Criterion-Referenced Tests

At the beginning of each chapter in this text, we clearly establish the competencies or skills you will have at the conclusion of the chapter. Our concern is not how well you do when compared to your fellow students, but whether or not you can exhibit the skills stated throughout the text;

therefore, this text employs a *criterion-referenced* approach. The major concern when using criterion referencing is to establish an objective, competency, or skill with an acceptable level of performance and then determine whether or not the student can do it. Rather than compare a student to other students, with this approach the teacher compares the student to a predetermined standard. In doing so, demonstrable skills are clearly established.

The basic point to remember here is that criterion-referenced tests are solely concerned with the ability of the student to accomplish a specific skill or objective at a competent level. It is important to note that this level is clearly established prior to the test. Additional reading on both norm and criterion-referenced tests is found in Gronlund (1974).

EXERCISE 1.2

Identify each of the functions listed below as characteristic of norm-referenced tests (n) or criterion-referenced tests (c). Then compare your answers with the ones given in the feedback section at the end of the chapter.

1. Determines whether or not a student is in the top 10 per cent or bottom 10 per cent of the group
2. Must have predetermined standards.
3. Skills must be clearly demonstrated at a predetermined level.
4. Students are compared to standards
5. Students are compared with other classmates or groups of students.
6. Students compete against each other
7. Theoretically, all students could make an A.
8. The student's standing within the group is clearly identified,
9. Generally, one finds an equal distribution of letter grades.

10. More commonly used when teaching for mastery, competency, or the acquisition of skills.

DETERMINING GRADES

Test Scores and Grades

In the previous section, we discussed the nature of norm-referenced and criterion-referenced test scores. For the former, the score establishes the student's relationship to a group, whereas the latter reflects performance with regard to a predetermined standard. In both cases, scores are a measurement function which provides the teacher with data regarding the success of the planned objectives and the implementation of the unit of study. Assigning grades is an evaluation function because it is the teacher's responsibility to make judgments based upon these test scores and other data.

Methods for Determining Grades

When concerned with the student's standing within a group, teachers frequently employ the normal curve. Students interested in further exploring curves, central tendencies, and other statistics are referred to Smith and Adams (1972). Such a curve is appropriately used when the group is large and diversified, with the measurements lending themselves to that group. When this is the case, the teacher can expect to have 3.5 per cent *As*, 23.8 per cent *Bs*, 45 per cent *Cs*, 23.8 per cent *Ds*, and 3.5 per cent *Fs*. It is obvious that, when this system is used, some students must get *As* and some must fail, with a large number always doing *C* or average work.

Often, teachers are uncomfortable with the normal curve because there is a lack of flexibility; however, they are still interested in comparing students in a group. These teachers frequently employ the "eyeball method" which calls for the exercise of judgment in determining clusters of grades and breaks between the clusters.

When using this method, you must set up all the scores on a horizontal line and then examine them. This procedure is shown in Figure 1.1.

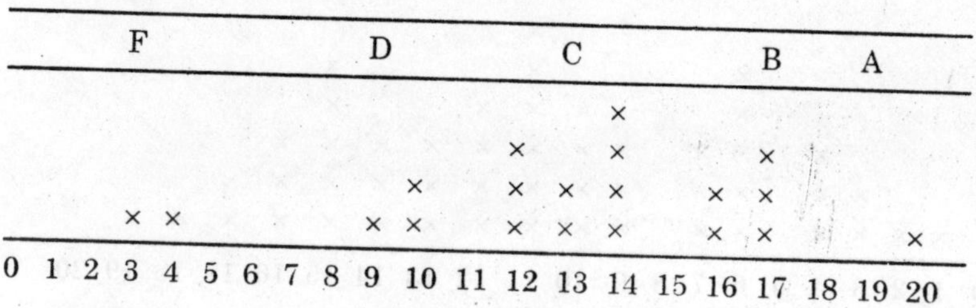

Figure 1.1 The "Eyeball Method"

It is possible that this will not yield *A* or *F* grades. If the highest score in Figure 1.2 had been 17, most teachers would not have assigned a grade of *A* for this work.

When concerned with student achievement measured against a predetermined standard, most teachers employ a percentage system. Over a period of time, the teacher determines an expectation in terms of student performance. For instance, the teacher may come to the conclusion that, when teaching first-grade students the addition of two-digit numbers, the student should be able to solve at least 16 out of 20 such problems on a paper and pencil test. In doing so, the teacher is clearly convinced that the student has mastered this skill or competency. Therefore, with regard to this particular example, a score of 80 percent or above would show the teacher and parent, as well as the student, that an acceptable level of performance had been achieved. For further study, including simple standard deviations, see Pierce and Lorber (1977).

EXERCISE 1.3

Answer the following questions for each of the groups of scores shown below. Then compare your answers to the ones given in the feedback section at the end of the chapter.

1. Using the normal curve percentages, how many students in this sample would receive A's?

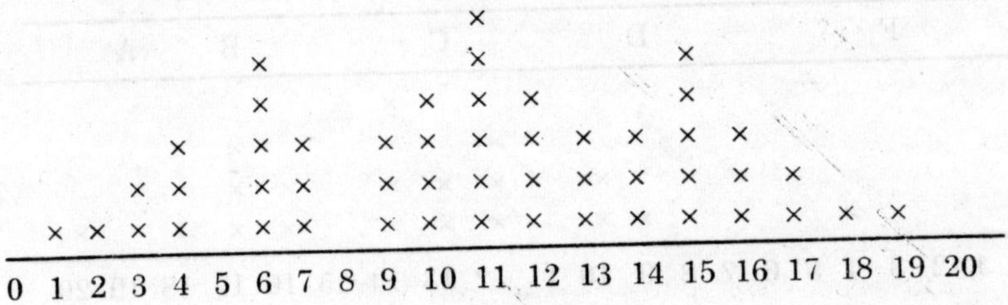

2. Using the "eyeball method," determine the letter grades *A, B, C, D* and *F* for the sample below :

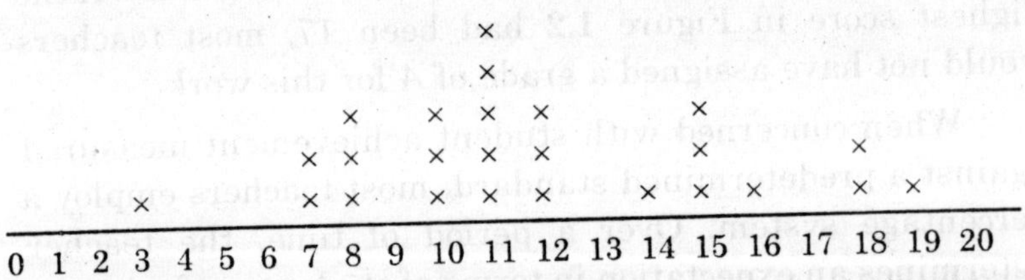

3. Using the percentage method and a pass/fail letter grade system (with 80 per cent being acceptable performance), how many of the following scores are passing?

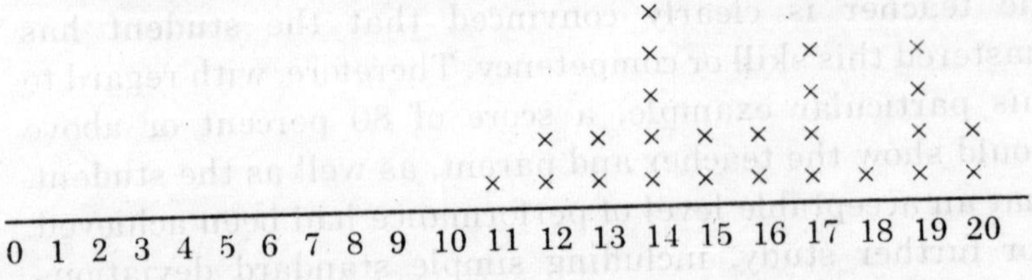

PURPOSES FOR GIVING GRADES

Feedback

First and foremost, grades provide feedback for students and parents. In doing so, a grade becomes an indicator of achievement or performance in a given unit or course of study. If such feedback is to be of any use, the students and their parents should be familiar with the grading system. The most common is the letter grade system which utilizes *A*, *B*, *C*, *D*, and *F* grades. These letters have more or less represented *excellent, good, average, poor*, and *failing* respectively.

In some areas, you might encounter a Pass/Fail (P/F) or an Honors/Satisfactory/Unsatisfactory system (H/S/U). Whatever the system being used, its purpose is to communicate the educational progress of the pupil. Alcorn, Kinder, and Shunert (1970) present an excellent review of feedback systems.

This knowledge of progress is very critical for it allows teachers to monitor the strengths and weaknesses of a student regarding a specific objective. This in turn serves as a guide for further course work. An *A* is an indicator that the student is most likely strong in that area and may be ready to move ahead, engage in enrichment exercises, or help a peer who is having difficulty with the material, A letter grade of *D* or *F* shows that the original instruction may not have met the student's need and that additional or alternative strategies or materials may be needed to advance the student to an acceptable level of performance.

When grades provide feedback of a highly positive or successful nature, they may serve as an incentive or motivational factor. Much research is being devoted to mastery learning which is a highly success-oriented method of instruction. Increased numbers of students in mastery environments appear to be making increases in cognitive achievement, and some of the research is focusing on the success factor which may be fostering additional successful experiences. Mastery Learning may also show that even negative feedback can promote learning if undertaken in a nonthreatening, nongraded fashion. In other words, not all feedback need be positive nor in the form of a grade.

Other Uses for Grades

Grades are used not only to provide feedback to parents and students but also for a wide range of institutional needs. They are one of a number of factors used as a basis for grouping students. If a grade truly reflects achievement, it is legitimate to use such information when assigning students to math and reading groups at the elementary level and advanced or specialized courses at the high school level.

Needless to say, grades are used by school systems to promote students from one grade level to the next and to graduate students from different levels within the system. Grades are often used to determine honor students and often serve as the basis for awards and scholarships. They may even determine whether or not a student is eligible to engage in extra curricular activities. Finally, grades are a major factor regarding college admission or job selection thereby serving as a force which goes beyond the school.

Although the original purpose of grades was to provide information regarding student progress and achievement, there can be little doubt that as educational institutions have grown, grades have become a potentially critical factor to the success in the adult world of today's students. This is true not only in the professions but also in any area which requires the student to exhibit mastery of a skill. For additional reading in this area, the student is referred to Alexander (In Beckner, Weldon, Dumas, 1968).

EXERCISE 1.4

In the spaces provided below, list three purposes for determining grades. Then check your answers with the ones given in the feedback section at the end of the chapter

1. ______________________________

____

____

____

2. ______________________________

____

____

____

3. ______________________________

____

____

____

Inappropriate Uses for Grades

As stated previously, the most critical purpose of grades is that of serving as an indicator of achievement by being the vehicle to communicate this achievement to students and their parents. However, there are many other ways in which grades are used in classrooms.

Frequently; a higher, inappropriate grade is assigned to a student whose achievement has been low but whose effort has been high. In this way, the function is that of an incentive to keep trying regardless of the degree of achievement. When this takes place, the grade becomes more important than the achievement, which is most often undesirable. The problem which arises from this situation is that a student might have solid grades yet very low scores on the standardized measurements, a situation which confuses and frustrates parents and aggravates administrations and school boards.

If the function of a grade is to transmit information regarding student achievement, one must avoid communicating inaccurate information such as would be done by assigning a grade higher than was earned. The teacher should also avoid using grades as a management axe. If a student achieves at the *B* level, it is illogical to report *C* achievement because of a lack of participation, poor attendance, or a management/discipline problem. Those situations should be handled in other ways as discussed earlier in the text.

Affective areas must also be communicated in other ways. Grades should not be used to help a student maintain a positive self-concept or help him move away from a negative one. Grades should not be given to reward the cooperative nor to punish the uncooperative student.

The best way to support students is to continually review and upgrade the quality of instruction which will allow increased numbers of students to achieve academically which will then be reflected in higher grades,

EXERCISE 1.5

With regard to the list below, place an *X* in front of the statements which reflect appropriate functions of grades. Then compare your answers with the ones given in the feedback section at the end of the chapter.

1. Grades should be awarded for effort.
2. Grades should be awarded to support a positive self-concept.
3. Grades should be awarded to help students conquer a negative self-concept.
4. Grades should accurately transmit academic achievement.
5. Grades could be lowered based upon participation and attendance.

FEEDBACK SYSTEMS

Feedback to Students

Students receive feedback from teachers on a daily basis in many ways. One of the most common is that of a grade on a formal measurement such as a paper and pencil test. As stated earlier, the meaning of the grade must be clear and easily understood by the student so that it clearly communicates the level of achievement. Of course, teachers are always writing comments on papers and providing verbal feedback. Again the major point to be made is that all feedback regarding communication of achievement must be comprehensible.

In addition, the teacher's grading policies and system should be simple and clear to the student. As we have emphasized throughout this hook, students have a right to know their learning situations and the objectives they are expected to meet. They must know at what level they must perform in order for them to succeed. Feedback regarding performance and achievement should be continuous, and the student should know of his standing at all times. The "secret stuff" has gone on for too long; teachers must take the guesswork out of grades and grading schemes.

Feedback to Parents

The most common form of communicating grade's to parents is the report card. The high school report card offers grades which should be reflections of academic achievement while the elementary report card serves the same function in addition to providing information on satisfactory or unsatisfactory performance in other, non academic areas.

The parents should be familiar with as much performance information as the school can provide, most often presented in the form of grades. However, this information must be useable by clearly communicating levels of achievement. A letter grade of *B* in one class might not mean the same as a *B* of another class. As mentioned earlier, parents seeing satisfactory grades on report cards and low percentiles on standardized tests fail to understand how this can happen.

What teachers must keep in mind is that the reason for a report card or any other communication device is to increase parents' awareness of the educational progress of their children. The report card is only one way of achieving this goal.

Another method of communicating progress is a written report. Such reports should be clear, easy to read, and void of any grade reporting as such. In everyday language, the teacher must communicate the general academic situation, being concerned with not only what he is trying to say but also with the way he is trying to say it.

The most effective way of communicating with parents is through a conference. Face-to-face, verbal communication allows the parent to ask questions and the teacher to provide understandable information. As stated earlier, parents need to know what grades mean, and in a conference, the teacher can very clearly discuss observable achievement as well as learning difficulties. The teacher should also realize that the parent conference is a two-way street and provides the opportunity to gain increased and valuable information about the student and his home environment. Such information may become instrumental in helping the teacher promote further achievement.

EXERCISE 1.6

Which of the following three reporting systems is the most effective: report cards, written reports, or parent conferences. Give two reasons for your choice. Then compare your answers with the ones given in the feedback section at the end of the chapter

Most effective reporting system:

1. ______________________________________
   ____

2. ______________________________________
   ____

Parents and the Affective Domain

During the 1970s, mastering the basics became the publicly proclaimed goal of American education. Although the zealousness of individuals committed to this effort has abated somewhat, "back to the basics" continues to dominate modern curriculums. Nevertheless, the majority of today's professional educators enthusiastically support the concept of educating the "whole child."

A significant component of this concept involves the affective domain. As you know from your reading of Chapter 2, it is in this area that teachers provide educational opportunities for students to express and share values, attitudes, feelings, opinions, and a variety of viewpoints. It is in this area that students become more aware of their surroundings, exhibit the willingness to listen to varying positions, and choose to become actively involved in the educational environment.

Needless to say, affective units of instruction have become somewhat controversial in the public sector and are particularly so when labelled with such concepts as the humanistic curriculum and values clarification.

Based upon the assumptions that (1) affective units are essential to the "whole child" concept and (2) affective units can stimulate parental involvement, teachers need to consider coping behaviours regarding parental attitudes toward the affective domain.

In line with most management-type situations, teachers should first consider preventive strategies, methods, and approaches. They should anticipate conflicts with parents and be as prepared, in advance, as possible. Points for consideration here include:

Using state and district-adopted materials

Providing parents with opportunities for suggesting topics

Checking in advance with potentially sensitive parents

Utilizing guidance counsellors

Guiding the discussions

Establishing a rationale for the activity

Securing the backing of chairpersons or team leaders

Securing administrative approval

Avoiding discussions regarding specific classroom individuals

Focusing on situations

Utilizing indirect teaching approaches such as questioning and paraphrasing

Stressing the ground rule that all opinions are acceptable with regard to the discussion

Stressing that overt participation is not required

Increasing knowledge of students' backgrounds

Introducing many points of view

Having thorough lesson plans

Serving in the role of a facilitator

Delimiting influence

Providing parents with outlines and descriptions of exercises.

Assuming that preventives may, on occasion, fall short, teachers must anticipate face-to-face meetings with parents (regarding a component of the affective domain with which the parents is displeased) and should consider ways of minimizing conflicts. Suggestions here include:

Being courteous and explaining your rationale

Listening to the parents' point of view

Discussing the situation frankly and supporting positions with policies

Bringing in outside support in the form of colleagues, counsellors, and administrators

Discussing alternatives

Focusing on the child

Having a third party present

Being prepared to professionally defend your curriculum

Inviting parents to observe the class

Being friendly and concerned

Establishing the value of the exercise

Being positive about the impact of the exercise

Being prepared to cite possible solutions

Understanding and respecting the parents

Using records to support the curriculum

Having sample techniques available

Documenting meetings with parents.

Finally, a published set of administrative guidelines, which could be made available to parents as well as faculties, can do much to enhance effective communication, provide focal points for discussion and, to some degree, educate the public about the process and value of affective units. Such guidelines might include defining exercises as a non threatening communications process for helping students understand positive or negative consequences of holding interests, attitudes, and beliefs; directing exercises toward the teaching of decision-making skills based upon democratic, principles; requiring lesson plans for the purpose of administrative approval; and being sure activities are conducted by certified, professional employees who are trained and qualified to use affective processes.

In the long run, the key to the successful implementation of affective experiences in the classroom will be found in the professional educator's ability to assist parents in understanding the meaning of the affective domain and the value of having their children's total growth stimulated by such a learning environment.

EXERCISE 1.7

Read the following scenario and identify two ways in which the teacher attempted to prevent potential conflict with parents regarding a unit involving the affective domain.

Mr Larsen decided to design a unit of instruction on the nuclear disarmament issue. As always, he prepared his objectives and then began to select appropriate content, strategies, and materials that would facilitate the unit. He located some excellent materials suggested by the National Council for the Social Studies (NCSS). He also found a simulation which required the students to discuss their individual opinions regarding the nuclear disarmament issue. His principal assured him that it was an appropriate exercise within the unit He also located a rather controversial film on atomic warfare and decided it was too powerful to pass up. He further decided that all his students would watch the film and write a brief paper on their reactions to it. Finally, he decided to tie all the instructional activities to a series of penetrating problems and questions offered at the conclusion of the chapter on World War II in the students' state-adopted textbook. As was his custom, Mr. Larsen then set about the task of developing compatible measurements which would allow him to evaluate student progress.

____

____

____

____

____

____

In this chapter we've presented much of the third phase of the three-phase model of teachilng. We discussed the differences between measurement and evaluation and then focused on measurement accuracy.

The idea of measurement accuracy was devceloped around sample items designed to measure the production or recognition of facts, concepts, and generalizations. A detailed discussion of multiple choice items was woven into the description. We then closed this section with a brief introduction to the idea of measuring for inquiry skills.

A complete discussion of all the forms of measurement items, including various observational items, is beyond the scope of this text, and the reader wishing more information in this area should consult a text devoted primarily to measurement and evaluation.

The determining and communicating of grades, as discussed in this chapter, marks the last step of the three-phase model. When determining grades, teachers must first decide whether they are going to compare students to students or students to preset standards. Once this decision is made, the next step is to select an appropriate grading system which allows the teacher to objectively assign letter grades. It is important to note that a certain amount of subjectivity is always present, no matter how objective the grading system.

Once letter grades have been assigned, the next step is to clearly and understandably communicate them to students as well as parents. The critical point here is that the letter grade must accurately represent student performance. Once this step is accomplished, the utilization of the three-phase model is complete.

As a final point, it should be understood that using this model involves a never ending process. Although assigning and communicating grades completes the evaluation phase, the teacher must now examine student achievement in order to plan, implement, and evaluate subsequent instruction. Therefore, the utilization of the three-phase model is a circular situation in which the teacher is engaged in an endless instructional series. Only through such a process can teachers hope to improve instruction on a continual basis and thereby promote student achievement and a success-oriented environment .

As stated at the onset, it is our firm conviction that your utilization of the three-phase model as described throughout this work will enhance your effectiveness in the classroom.

However, we hasten to add that the conclusion of the three-phase model does not conclude the teaching act. On the contrary, it is merely a beginning in that your original planning, implementing, and evaluating—effective as it may have been—enables you to revisit the unit or lesson and revise your work by replanning, reimplementing, and re-evaluating.

We hope three-phase model will be invaluable to you in your efforts to maximize achilevement in the three areas (knowledge and information, attitudes and values, and manipulative skills) of student learning. The utilization of this neverending cycle truly marks the professional educator who continually strives to provide · learning experiences and a classroom environment that facilitates the growth of each and every child.

Exercise Feedback

EXERCISE A

In each of the items the students must, of course, be able to read. In addition they must be able to do or know the following:

1. A.

   (1) Be able to measure.
   (2) Know that $C = \pi d$ applies to this problem
   (3) Know the formula $C = \pi d$
   (4) Remember the value of π.
   (5) Know the relationship between radius and diameter.
   (6) Be able to put the numbers in the equation.
   (7) Be able to multiply decimals

   B.

   (1) Know that $C = \pi d$ applies to this problem.
   (2) Know the formula $C = \pi d$.
   (3) Remember the value of π.
   (4) Be able to put the numbers in the equation.
   (5) Be able to multiply decimals

   C.

   (1) Know the value of π
   (2) Be able to put the numbers in the equation.
   (3) Be able to multiply decimals.

From these lists we see item A is the most demanding. It requires more prerequisite site knowledge than either of the others. It is also the most realistic in that concrete examples of circles are in the item rather than making the students think about circles in the abstract.

2. A. Application

   B. Application

   C. Comprehension

   Both Items A and B are at the application level in that they both require the students to select the formula and calculate the circumference. Item A requires abilities such as measuring and knowing the relationship between radius and diameter that the teacher may not want to require. In order to capture realism, the teacher could rewrite. Item B as follows:

   Calculate the circumference of each of the following circles:

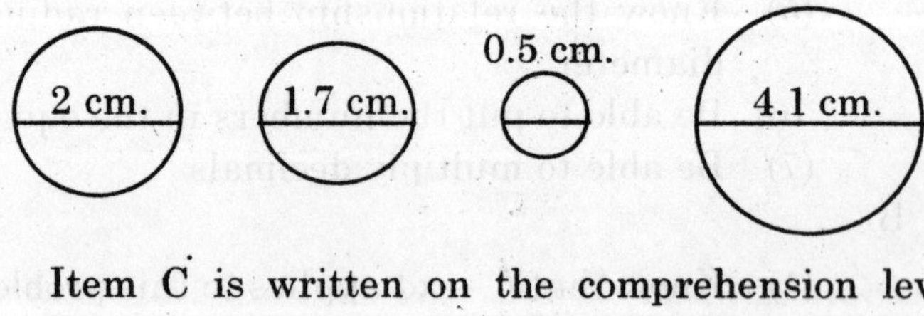

   Item C is written on the comprehension level because the equation was given, and the students only had to put the numbers in it and compute the result

3. A. Production

   B. Production

   C. Production

   Because the responses are convergent in each

case, production items are a better choice than recognition. However, a recognition item could have been written (although, of course, a different evaluation statement would have to appear with the goal statement in Mr. Hite's objective). A recognition item can be written as follows:

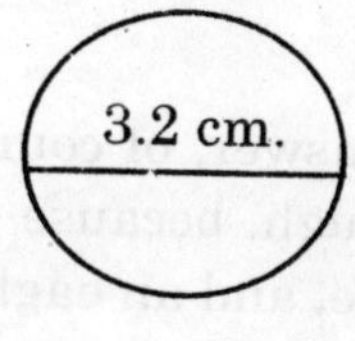

The circumference of the circle is

a. 1.6 cm.

b. 8.04 cm.

c. 10.05 cm.

d. 5.02 cm.

EXERCISE B

Item 2 is definitely better than Item 1. In Item 1 the correct choice is obvious since it is the only four-sided figure. In Item 2, the child must discriminate among four different four-sided figures. Also, he must know the difference between a rectangle and a square and between a rectangle and a trapezoid. A teacher could be quite certain the children had a concept of rectangle if they marked Item 2 correctly, while he might be mistaken with a correct response so Item 1.

EXERCISE C

The following would be an appropriate item to measure a small child's comprehension of the concept *mammal*. Of course, your item is probably somewhat different, but it should have good distracters

Circle the animal that is a mammal. (Assume this would be read to the students and that the four choices would be in pictorial form.)

a. Frog
b. Cow
c. Alligalor
d. Eagle

The correct answer, of course, is cow. The distracters are good ones, though, because a frog is an amphibian, an alligator is a reptile, and an eagle is a bird. Each represents a concept coordinate to the concept mammal and measures the child's ability to discriminate among coordinate concepts. (For a review of coordinate concepts refer to Chapter 2.1)

EXERCISE D

1. Comprehension. The students are asked to identify an illustration of the generalization
2. In order to respond correctly, students must relate smoking and heart disease,
   a. Heart disease but no smoking.
   b. Smoking but no heart disease.
   c. Correct—heart disease and smoking,
   d. Heart disease but no smoking.

If the distracters were written without any reference to either smoking or heart disease, the students could respond correctly without understanding the generalization. This would make the item invalid and could give the teacher some misinformation about student understanding.

EXERCISE E

The following is an item that could be used. In this case, as with many others in this chapter, there are a number of appropriate possibilities.

The Tahitians have a peaceful, fun-loving culture. Life in Tahiti hasn't changed much in the last hundred years. Many Tahitians still fish for a living. Because it is warm, many wear a sarong the year round just as their ancestors have for centuries.

The sentence that illustrates the generalization, climate affects culture is

a. Tahitians have a peaceful, fun-loving culture.
b. Life in Tahiti hasn't changed much in the last hundred years.
c. Many Tahitians still fish for a living.
d. Because it is warm, many wear a sarong the year round just as their ancestors have for centuries.

EXERCISE F

1. (ns) Does not support. The explanation says Group A people are slim, but, according to the data, their weight to height ratio is higher.
2. (s) Supports.
3. (ns) Does not support. The explanation says Group A people drink little but the data says they drink an average of four drinks per person per day.
4. (s) Supports.
5. (ns) Does not support. The explanation says Group B people breathe dirty air but the data says the city in which they live is noted for "soft" industry, which is nonpulluting.
6. (s) Supports
7. (ns) Does not support. The explanation says Group B people are sedentary, while the data says they exercise.

8. (ns) Does not support. The explanation says Group A people avoid harmful items like tobacco, while the data says they smoke
9. (s) Supports
10. (s) Supports

EXERCISE G

1. (e) Evaluation. A decision was made based on some previous measurement.
2. (fm) Formal Measurement. Miss Anthony consciously planned to gather some information about her students and did so by checking to see if they could match similar first sounds.
3. (e) Evaluation.
4. (e) Evaluation.
5. (im) Informal Measurement. The teacher, in an unplanned way gathered some information
6. (im) Informal Measurement.
7. (e) Evaluation
8. (im) Informal Measurement.
9. (e) Evaluation.

EXERCISE H

1. (n) Norm-referenced. With criterion-referenced tests, bottom and top percents are not identified.
2. (c) Criterion-referenced.
3. (c) Criterion-referenced.
4. (c) Criterion-referenced.
5. (n) Norm-referenced.
6. (n) Norm-referenced. The highest scores receive a letter grade of A and the lowest a letter grade of F.
7. (c) Criterion-referenced. If the highest score, based upon 100 per cent, was 99 per cent and the lowest was 95 per cent, all might be awarded the letter grade of A.

8. (n) Norm-referenced.
9. (n) Norm - referenced. The usual grade distribution is mostly the letter grade of C with some Bs and Ds and a few As and Fs.
10. (c) Criterion - referenced. These approaches require the establishment of predetermined standards.

EXERCISE I

1. 2. There are fifty scores in the sample. The top 3.5 per cent of the scores are to be awarded As. Therefore, $0.035 \times 50 = 1.75$ or approximately two students
2. A—scores 18-19
   B—scores 14-16
   C—scores 10-12
   D—scores 7-8
   F—score 3
3. 13. A passing score would be 80 per cent of 20 or $0.80 \times 20 = 16$. Therefore, any score of 16 or over, of which there are 13, would be awarded a passing letter grade

EXERCISE J

Any of the following would be acceptable responses:

1. Inform students of educational progress
2. Inform parents of educational progress.
3. Guide further course work.
4. Provide a basis for grouping.
5. Provide a basis for promoting.
6. Provide a basis for graduating.
7. Provide a basis for college admission.
8. Provide a criterion for honors.
9. Provide a criterion for extra-curricular participation.

10. Provide a motivational factor.
11. Identify student strengths and weaknesses.
12. Provide a basis for employment.

EXERCISE K

1. No X
2. No X.
3. No X.
4. X.
5. No X. If the grade accurately reflects student achievement, there can be no legitimate reason for lowering the grade. However, teachers often build participation and attendance into their grading scheme

EXERCISE L

The most effective reporting system is the parents conference. Any two of the following are acceptable reasons:

1. Allows parents questions and teacher answers.
2. Allows parents to learn exactly what a grade means.
3. Allows the teacher to explain both progress and problems.
4. Allows the teacher to learn more about the student and his home environment.

EXERCISE M

1. Mr. Larsen secured the approval of his principal.
2. Mr. Larsen used a state-adopted textbook.

   NOTE: Mr. Larsen may have been encouraging some difficulty in the following ways:

   1. He used materials that had not been approved.

2. He required all students to participate in an overt way.

References

Alcorn, M, Kinder, J., & Shunert, J. (1970). *Better teaching in secondary school*. New York: Holt, Rinehart & Winston.

Anderson, R. (1972). How to construct achievement tests to assess comprehension. *Review of Educational Research*, 42, 145-70.

Beckner, W., & Dumas, W. (Eds).. (1968). *Readings in secondary education*. Scranton, PA: International Textbook Company.

Brown, J. (Ed.). (1976). *Recall and recognition*, New York: John Wiley.

Crow, L., & Crow, A. (Eds.). (1964), *Vital issues in American education*. New York: Bantam.

Ebel, R. (1970). *Essentials of educational measurements*. Englewood Cliffs, NJ: Prentice-Hall.

Gronlund, N. (1968). *Constructing achievement tests*. Englewood Cliffs, NJ: Prentice-Hall.

Gronlund, N. (1974), *Improving marking and reporting in classroom instruction*. New York: Macmillan.

Jackson, P. (1968). *Lift in classrooms*. New York: Holt. Rinehart & Winston.

Ladas, H., & Postman, N. (1974). Grades: Standardizing the unstandardized standard. *Phi Delta Kappan*, 56, 185-88.

Lindvall, C. M., & Nitko, A. (1975). *Measuring pupil achievement and aptitude*. New York: Harcourt Brace Jovanovich.

Lyman, H. (1978). *Test scores and what they mean*. Englewood Cliffs, NJ: Prentice-Hall.

Mager, R. (1973). *Measuring instructional intent*. Belmont. CA: Fearon.

Manning, D, (1971). *Toward a humanistic curriculum*. New York: Harper & Row.

Pierce, W., & Lorber, M. (1977). *Objectives and methods for secondary teaching*. Englewood Clifs, Nj: Prenice-Hall.

Schoer, L, (1970), *Test construction: A programmed guide*. Boston: Allyn & Bacon.

Simon, S., & Bellanca, J. (Eds.). (1976). *Degrading the grading myths: A primer of alternatives to grades and marks*. Washington, D.C: Association for Supervision and Curriculum Development.

Smith, F., & Adams, S, (1972). *Educational measurement for the classroom teacher*. New York; Harper & Row.

Wickelgren, W. (1977). *Learning and memory*. Englewood Cliffs, NJ: Prentice-Hall.

2
Evaluation and Assessment

It may be helpful to begin by offering a distinction between 'evaluation' and 'assessment' in education. The distinction is a fairly conventional one, not intended to be definitive or provocative, but simply to avoid confusion within the compass of this article. The .purpose of assessment is to make statements about the recipients of an educational service, statements about their actual and potential accomplishments in relation to the opportunities for learning provided by that service. Assessment is the basis for decisions about what students will get in the way of further provision, and for predictions of their future accomplishments. The purpose of evaluation, on the other hand, is not to make statements about the recipients, but to make statements about the educational service. Evaluation statements serve decisions about educational *provision*. It will be obvious that assessment can assist this purpose, and that some form of assessment is a likely component of any evaluation process. True enough, but the distinction by primary purpose is more significant than may at first sight appear to be the case.

The fact is that the instruments of assessment that we have laboriously cultivated and refined over the years the examination procedures and the psychometric tests, are not much help to the educational evaluator. Such instruments are typically constructed so as to differentiate between the accomplishments of individual learners, that is, to achieve a distribution of scores. These instruments are known as norm-referenced, because they make it possible to rank the individual in relation to the performance of the group. This discrimination facilitates educational and vocational placement. But assessment for the purpose of evaluation calls for a different approach, because it is asking different questions. What did the students need to learn? Given the nature of the provision for learning, the circumstances of its implementation, and the intentions of the teachers, what could they reasonably have been expected to learn? What did they *all* learn and what did they all fail to learn? Instruments which set out to answer these kinds of questions require *criteria* rather than norms as their design basis. They are known as criteria-referenced, and they have an important function in the evaluation of educational programmes. The massive task of constructing such criterion-referenced tests which are reliable and valid is only now getting underway. Very few are readily available in this country at the present time, and this in part explains why during the last decade, evaluators have increasingly adopted and developed approaches to their task which place little emphasis on the measurement of student performance. I shall have more to say about this later: it is enough for the moment to have established that evaluation and assessment, as I have defined them, have different purposes and that, even though they share an interest in student learning, they require different instruments.

The Context of Evaluation — Values

But I don't want this article to be primarily a technological review of the province of evaluation. The rising demand for evaluation in education (and I think it wiser to talk of 'demand' rather than 'popularity') calls instead for a much broader consideration of the circumstances which surround this demand. Evaluation can so easily be an instrument of abuse that the context in which it's applied should always be carefully scrutinized. 'Who's Afraid of Evaluation?' the title of this article, is offered in a spirit of caution rather than contempt.

These are troubled times in education, are they not? The air is shrill with criticism, threats, challenges; war cries of one kind and another. Some of the rather sloganized exchanges that characterize the public debate have been with us for some time, and are familiar enough — formal *versus* informal teaching methods, comprehensivization *versus* selection, streaming *versus* mixed ability, and so on. They may have sharpened in tone of late, but we know them well. In a sense, many of us feel that much of this debate lies outside education, although it is about education. What actually happens within the schools is determined still by the values and preferences of those most intimately involved in educational provision — headmaster, teachers, and local administrators. This degree of autonomy in matters of curriculum provision, although a thorough analysis would no doubt qualify it in a number of ways, has been sufficiently substantial for us to feel that the affairs of the school are under professional control, and that this arrangement enjoys public confidence. Can we still say that today? I think not, and I have in mind not only the effects of the economic disaster which has overtaken educational expenditure and which I shall come to shortly, but of other trends and events whose effects are rather more difficult to calculate. Events like the William Tyndale saga, which culminated in an inconclusive three-month-long 'evaluation', and which raised a number of issues that are much less familiar than the 'chestnuts' referred to earlier. Tyndale was an event which compelled the confrontation of long dormant issues in education in the light of contemporary trends. For instance, who is accountable for educational provision, to whom, and by what means? And, if a pluralist society entails a pluralist teaching profession, what are the implications for the school as an agency of cultural transmission? To put this last question more baldly, can schools still be relied upon to reinforce the existing social order? The 'problem school' in this sense is a new phenomenon, one which many people link with the inner urban crisis of recent years, as well as with a general growth of political consciousness within the educational community. The extent to which Tyndale, and its successors, leads to an erosion of public confidence in the schools may well depend on the extent to which it is seen as an opportunity to change the existing distribution of power within the education system. The *Times Educational Supplement* saw in the actions of the parents of Tyndale the emergence of a new tide of educational 'consumerism'. The ILEA followed the inquiry by appointing a new group of inspectors to monitor school standards. The DBS reinforced its recent call for a national monitoring system. There is, at least incipiently, a sense of crisis in the air, and a tendency to respond by seeking strong measures to re-establish control. Whereas Rising Hill was seen by its critics as an aberration, Tyndale has been interpreted as an early warning signal.

The Context of Evaluation — Efficiency

If cultural fragmentation is one context which gives rise to calls for closer monitoring of the school system, inept management of resources is another. During the 'seventies' we have seen, both at the national level and the local level, a significant change in the model of resource management applied to educational expenditure. Using techniques and procedures evolved primarily in industry and defence, the planners in Elizabeth House have designed, and are seeking ways to apply, a system of management which involves a shift from input to output budgeting, a system which calls for evaluation of the effects of alternative resource allocations in relation to objectives and costs. To put into operation such a system requires the cooperation of the planners at local level, and since 1971, there has been considerable exploration of the integration problems of local and national planning (see *Management in the Education Service: Challenge and Response* an SEO occasional paper published in 1974). The reorganization of local government in 1974 gave an immediate, and perhaps crucial, boost to the new model of management, introducing as it did the 'corporate management' structure. Corporate management involves the formation of cross-departmental executive committees, horizontal movement of staff at senior management level, and a strong emphasis on policy evaluation of a kind that is required if the aspirations of the Department planners are to be fulfilled. Now, at the local as well as the national level, we have a commitment to goal-setting and the evaluation of goal attainment. The new power structure of local authorities ensures that Education, the 'big spender', will come under pressure to justify its resources in terms of demonstrable outcomes. Game, set and match to the men from the Ministry.

The New Rhetoric

Add to the foregoing contexts the economic recession and we begin to understand why the mood of optimism which imbued public discussion about curriculum development in the 'sixties', and the rhetoric of constructive support and cooperation that went with it, are sadly frayed. Now we hear, suddenly it seems, a new vocabulary of relatively unfamiliar terms, a vocabulary more militant in tone than we are accustomed to, more strident in advocacy than many of us feel comfortable with. Top of the list is the word 'accountability', a concept we used to associate with financial audits, but which is now applied to the processes find outcomes of schooling, and to the obligations of those who have responsibility for those processes and outcomes. Many other 'new' words we are being asked to learn seem, like accountability, to belong to the world of production organizations, words like 'cost benefit' 'efficiency', 'management by objectives', 'programme budgeting', 'control systems' and the 'like.' The tendency of language like this is to suggest that the production of educated people is much like the production of anything else, a technological problem of specification and manufacture. And, like the production of anything else, it can best be organized hierarchically, each part or subsystem dovetailing into a master plan which encompasses and orchestrates the whole organization.

In the case of education, specifying the product is the really tricky bit of the process. First of all, everyone in the organization must agree what the product is to be. To derive an analogy from car production, it's no use if some of the workers think it's a Mini while others think it's a Land Rover. Objectives must be pre-determined. Secondly there must be agreement about what the product will look like, how it will be identified. In education, this means that the objectives must be defined in terms of learner behaviour. And this is where another word enters the contemporary vocabulary, the word 'standards'. Not a new word of course, 'standards' is the traditional war cry of the educational 'right'. 'Standards' are what grammar schools stand for, what you get if you concentrate on the three Rs, what you lose when your hair touches the back of your neck or when you enter a comprehensive school. 'Standards' is the central construct of a familiar polemic at the political level of education policy disputes. But of late the concept has come more and more to be employed in its operational sense, as criteria of acceptable performance. When the Department of Education's newly fledged Assessment of Performance Unit talks of standards, it means levels of pupil achievement which can be used as the basis of a national monitoring system (Kay, 1974). In other words, specified behaviour objectives.

While it would be going too far to suggest that what is taking place is a transformation in the way that schooling is viewed as resource investment, it would be wrong, and dangerous, to dismiss this trend as mere verbal fashion unlikely to impinge in any significant way upon the activities of the school. The changing rhetoric of educational management reflects in a very direct way the transformation of the economic circumstances of schooling that has been wrought in the past few years.

It would be difficult to resist the proposition that the British educational system, and particularly the school system, is about to launch itself into a new phase, perhaps a decade, of unprecedented concern with evaluation. Unprecedented that is, in modern times: some of the rhetoric of the platform speakers bears a chilling resemblance to the remark of Robert Lowe, Vice-President of the Education Department, when, in 1861, he recommended to the House of Commons the issue of a 'revised code' which introduced the notorious and ill-fated system of 'payment by results' — 'If the new system is not cheap, it shall be efficient, and if it is not efficient, it shall be cheap.' In one sense, current rhetoric goes one step further. The context of Lowe's promise was one of rapidly expanding expenditure on schooling, which payment by results failed to stem. The context today is one of a declining resource future. The new system, therefore, has no options. It shall be efficient, and it shall be cheap.

Thus baldly stated, the demand represents a transformation of the social and political circumstances of the school, one which has materialized with bewildering rapidity. The demand is backed by fiscal control and made legitimate by public concern about 'standards'; it cannot with impunity be ignored. Already there are some ominous signs. The ailing National Foundation for Educational Research is showing all the signs of revival as orders for new tests come in from the Department, itself gratified by Bullock's call for national monitoring of reading standards. A change of role is planned for the HMIs who want the local advisers to take over much of their individual school inspection function, and it is interesting to note a change of nomenclature at the local level, where some former advisers are now called evaluators. And here come the volunteers. I note in a recent issue of the *Times Educational Supplement* that the principal of a College of Further Education has welcomed accountability in the form of an external audit. Who's afraid of evaluation?

Where does all this leave the school, and the evaluators, whoever they may be? The context which I have attempted to outline suggests that future evaluation efforts in the schools are likely to arise out of, and feedback into, a centralized system of performance monitoring based on pre-set targets. We should note several salient features of this system. In the first place, viewed as an accountability system, it is clear that some are more accountable than others. The Department of Education and Science for instance, though part of what Margaret Thatcher called the least accountable bureaucracy in Western Europe, and though it has led the crusade for accountability, is not offering to render its own operations and accomplishments more open to scrutiny. Of course the management model does in theory render the Department more accountable to its political masters but if one believes, with Professor Vaizey, that such accountability has 'vanished, even as a pretence' (Vaizey, 1974), and if one adds to this Tyrell Burgess's view that the effect of corporate management is to make 'it harder than ever for the representatives to control the officials' (in the *Guardian* May 7, 1974), then we face the possibility of an accountability system which only bites at the level of the schools. In the second place, the model of evaluation which is being advocated is extremely rudimentary and simplistic, one which no professional evaluator working in this country today would try to defend. Evaluation as the measurement of pupil attainment of pre-specified objectives is an excellent instrument for the purpose of central control of education, but a poor instrument of quality assurance, and an even poorer instrument for increasing understanding of the problems and potentials of educational provision. It is a bureaucratic concept of evaluation for a bureaucratic concept of accountability. Let the buyer beware. Earnest House has observed, in relation to the enactment of comparable accountability procedures in America, 'I believe such schemes are simplistic, unworkable, contrary to empirical findings, and ultimately immoral.' They are likely to lead to suspicion, acrimony, inflexibility, cheating, and finally control — which I believe is their purpose (House, 1973).

However we do not need to postulate malign intentions in order to predict malign effects and indeed would be unjustified in doing so. Few would deny that schools should be accountable, more so than they have been in the past, and most of us would support the need for more systematic study of alternatives in educational provision — their values, their processes, their circumstances and their effects. But there are many ways to be accountable, many audiences with legitimate claims for information, and different notions of what constitutes educational excellence. Evaluators increasingly acknowledge these propositions in their designs, which have moved away from simple output measurement in an effort to portray for decision-makers and others the complexity of the relationships between actions, circumstance, and consequence in educational affairs. It is this complexity that is in danger of being ignored if we subscribe to a form of evaluation that places overmuch reliance on a single productivity index, an index which, as I pointed out at the beginning of this artilcle, is underpinned by an undeveloped technology.

One final point: to judge schools by what we can measure in pupils is to judge them by our instruments, not by our heads or by our varying values. Ledger-book evaluation may lead us to assign false priorities undue emphasis in our provision. These recent words of Robert Stake are worth bearing in mind; The world encourages a great variety of competences across persons and tolerates a great incompetence in persons. Poor achievement is not despicable (though failure to provide opportunity for better achievement is). Poor achievement is often the scapegoat focus-of-attention when a person is rejected really because of social class, race, personality, or appearance. The incompetences of the handsome rich are greatly tolerated. a successful life is possible for any person with any combination of talents. With a heavy accent on low competence in certain academic areas, the schools can help deny a person the ordinary opportunities of a successful life (Stake, 1976).

And what of those who hold that education is characterized by indeterminacy of ends, anyway? Who's afraid of evaluation? I am , are you?

References

House, E. (1973) 'The price of productivity: Who pays?' published in mimeo by the University of Illinois.

Kay, B. (1975) 'Monitoring pupils' performance' *Trends in Education* July.

Stake, R. (1976) 'Measuring achievement in the schools' published in mimeo by the University of Illinois.

Vaizey, J. (1974) 'Expansion and contraction' *Times Educational Supplement* 28, June.

3
Education and School-based Evaluation

In educational discussion, it is often claimed that standards are declining and that progressive methods of teaching are wholly or partly the cause. In this article I want to look first of all at the issues which surround these two claims and ask 'what are they really about?'. Secondly, I shall look at the development of monitoring and accountability systems as a political and administrative response to these issues. In particular I hope to show that the development of accounting procedures for teachers and schools based on the monitoring of pupil achievements is inconsistent with the ideals of progressive education. Finally, I want to outline an alternative model of public accountability which is school—rather than bureaucratically—based and likely to be more acceptable to progressive educators.

The Issues about Standards

Both the issue about declining standards and that about causal responsibility appear on an initial inspection to be about the facts. But, in asserting that standards are declining, people are not simply asserting a fact but making a value judgment. The factual component amounts to 'standards are changing'. The evaluative component amounts to 'the changes are undesirable'. Now those who disagree may not disagree with the fact that 'standards are changing' but with the evaluation that 'the changes are undesirable'. In which case the question at issue is 'What sort of things are worth learning?'.

In asserting that progressive methods are the, or partial, cause of declining standards the traditionalist is in part making a claim about the observable facts; namely, that the adoption of such methods is normally sufficient, or along with other factors sufficient, to bring about a change in educational standards. However, causal statements about social situations cannot simply be reduced to observational statements. There are usually a large number of factors operating which are sufficient to bring about the occurrence one is concerned about. Why then, does the traditionalist select progressive methods as the, or a partial, cause of declining standards rather than some other factor or factors whose presence would be sufficient to bring about a decline?

Robert Ennis (1973) has argued that we select a particular factor as the, or a partial, cause in order to ascribe blame for the occurrence we are interested in. Thus, to assert that progressive methods are causally responsible for a decline in standards is not merely to state a fact based on observation but to attribute blame for the decline to these methods and those who adopt them.

In answering the traditionalist, the progressive educator need not disagree about the observable facts. He may admit that a change from traditional to progressive methods has accompanied a change of standards and even agree that this latter change is undesirable. But without being at all inconsistent he can deny that progressive methods are the, or a partial, cause by claiming that some other factor or factors are operating causally, for example, large classes, inadequate resources, low pupil motivation, low socio-economic status of parents. In doing so, he attributes blame to these other factors and thereby attempts to exonerate progressive methods and teachers. He can keep on citing such factors; the factual evidence will never be conclusive.

Faced with continually inconclusive factual evidence, the traditionalist may try another line of argument. 'Do you admit that a return to traditional methods would prevent or help to prevent a decline in standards?', he asks the progressive. 'I have already admitted it', replies the progressive. 'Well, since teachers have a responsibility, a duty, to maintain standards, shouldn't they abandon progressive methods and return to traditional ones?', the traditionalist pleads, 'I disagree that teachers should accept responsibility for what their pupils learn. Their main responsibilities are for the way they make provision for learning; for the quality of the learning environment. As teachers we are under no obligation to sacrifice the quality of the learning environment for the sake of maintaining achievement levels. Quantity may have to be sacrificed for quality', the progressive argues.

This fabricated dialogue illustrates something which lies at the heart of the issue about the causal responsibility of progressive methods for declining standards; namely, the responsibilities which go with being a teacher. In my dialogue, the traditionalist selects progressive teaching methods as the, or a, cause for declining standards because he assumes that a teacher's primary responsibility is for what pupils learn. On the other hand, the progressive teacher denies that progressive methods are causally responsible because he assumes that a teacher's main responsibility is for the way he teaches. A teacher is accountable for the things he has responsibilities for, so there is no way of arriving at a rational consensus on the accountability question if there is no rational procedure for resolving disagreemens about the nature of these responsibilities.

Achievement Testing and Accountability: The Official Response

As in the United States, so in the UK, the official response to public concern about standards has been an attempt to establish procedures for monitoring achievement levels in the form of an 'Assessment of Performance Unit' at the DES. This development appears at first sight to be rather more sophisticated in its approach than some of its counterparts in the USA, though like them it relies on the notion of consultative procedures to arrive at a consensus to guide the Unit's activities.

In an article the APU in *Education 3-13* Brian Kay the APU's first director, returns repeatedly to the problem of consensus, and appears to be rather irritated by the lack of it. For example, he expresses the hope that the Unit and its working groups 'can escape the tendency to polarize which bedevils much of our educational thinking and though to a lesser degree, educational practice' (1976). He argues that consensus is possible because 'there is a solid core of sound educational practice which follows a middle way' and adds, 'This seems to offer a serviceable starting point for our work'. What a quick way of reaching a consensus about standards. One simply excludes discussing those views which too radically conflict with one another. Such a neat political device may be a quick way of reaching a consensus; it could hardly fail. But it is hardly a good way of reaching a *rational consensus* based on a consideration of alternative views. The desire for consensus at any price tends to characterize politicians and officials who want to resolve social conflict primarily by technical means. Value-pluralism for them is just an embarrassment and the quicker it can be 'resolved' the better.

Dialogue is the method for trying to resolve rationally those fundamental issues which lie outside the realm of empirical proof. It proceeds by exploring alternative views and arguments; it does not push them to one side for the sake of a quick consensus. But it is dialogue which is threatened by the emergence of monitoring and accountability procedures at the bureaucratic level. The emergence of such procedures at the present time is evidence of increasing bureaucratic and political intrusion into life in our social institutions: a form of control which not only threatens dialogue within and between these institutions but the foundations of democracy itself. As I understand it, 'a democratic society' is a society in which social conflict is to be treated as a subject for dialogue among the people rather than an object of political and bureaucratic control. The bureaucratic development of 'consultative procedures' for determining standards is no real aid to democracy. Such procedures are inimical to dialogue because in the last resort a consensus on norms and values has to be reached for the sake of technical considerations.

In the USA, standardized achievement tests have been used as the basis for calling teachers and schools to account for declining standards. Such a use assumes that teachers have a responsibility to maintain and improve achievement levels. But judging from research such as that by Start (1974) and Jackson (1968), it appears that many teachers see themselves as having a responsibility for the quality of the classroom climate in which pupils learn rather than for what they learn. This doesn't mean such teachers are necessarily unconcerned about what pupils learn. It is not inconsistent for a teacher to have certain pupil achievements in mind as goals for his teaching but to deny at the same time that he can accept responsibility for their attainment. One reason why he may refuse to accept responsibility for pupil achievements is that the factors which influence achievement levels are difficult to control and it is not always within his power to prevent declining standards. Thus he will do his best to maintain and raise achievement levels but is not prepared to accept responsibility in these respects.

This sort of objection doesn't involve radical disagreement over values. The disagreement is primarily a factual one about the limits of teachers' powers to control achievement levels. In other words, can teaching reasonably be viewed as a sufficient condition for declining standards? Another more radical objection to teachers accepting responsibility for pupil achievements is that to do so would be an infringement of their pupils' capacity to accept responsibility for their own learning, and that it is the protection and fostering of this capacity for rational autonomy which teachers are primarily responsible for.

It is this sort of objection which underlies the consistent denial of my fictitious progressive educator that progressive methods are causally responsible for declining standards. They cannot be causally responsible because the progressive teacher's responsibility to protect and foster the rational autonomy of the pupil is inconsistent with his accepting responsibility for what pupils achieve. As I have argued, in holding this view the progressive educator need not be unconcerned about achievement levels. He can accept responsibility for deciding what is worth learning in his classroom, but since pupils have the right to evaluate this decision he cannot accept responsibility for whether they learn what he decides is worthwhile. I do not see any conflict in principle between the progressive teacher holding particular pupil achievements in mind as goals and his ideal of rational autonomy so long as he doesn't accept a responsibility to ensure that his goals are achieved at any price. I know that some progressive educators would disagree with me but this is because I think they confuse a responsibility for deciding what is worth learning with a responsibility for ensuring that pupils learn it.

Brian Kay has denied that the national monitoring procedures developed by the APU will be used to judge individual teachers or schools. In *Education 3-13*, he argues that the APU 'represents part of the response of the DES to demands for greater accountability by the educational service for the resources it consumes' (Kay, 1976). It appears, therefore, that its monitoring procedures will operate at the level of the 'educational service as a whole'. What exactly is meant by 'the educational service' is not clear. Does he mean the teaching profession as a collective body or would he include LEA administrators and advisers, not to mention the DES itself? If he means 'the teaching profession' as a whole then the procedures developed are intended as a basis for *making judgments about teachers*, irrespective of the extent to which individual schools and teachers are anonymized.

Although the unit's work is not intended to have any direct effects on individual teachers and schools it is intended to affect them indirectly. One of these indirect effects is that it will act as a normative influence in getting teachers to assess their practice against 'the best standards'; these being defined in terms of pupil achievements. Kay puts it like this:

> If the educational process is monitored according
> to criteria which reflect the best current practices

> in encouraging pupils' development in language, mathematics, science, moral and aesthetic sensibility and physical expression and dexterity, then the general level of these may rise towards that of the best. This is why it is so vital that the criteria used should both reflect the best practice and be reasonably comprehensive.

Thus self-evaluation by individual teachers and schools is an anticipated indirect effect of the work of the unit. But notice that it is only to be encouraged on the basis of 'the best criteria' which will presumably be determined by the unit and reinforced by government policy. Earlier in his article, Kay expresses reservations about the *Times Educational Supplement's* suggestion that teachers and schools should develop their own methods of self-evaluation. He argues that 'at a time of change and experiment there is a need for a general debate to help in defining criteria of assessment. Many people would also ask that self-assessment should be complemented by some form of objective monitoring, based on a sampling process, if only as a moderating device'.

It seems that self-evaluation is only desirable when the following conditions obtain:

1. the criteria of evaluation are achievement criteria
2. the criteria represent a consensus view of the responsibilities of teachers and schools
3. it is moderated externally.

The first condition would rule out self-evaluation based on alternative conceptions of the responsibilities of teachers to that of 'responsibility for pupil achievement levels'. The second begs a whole lot of questions about how the consensus is reached; questions I raised earlier. The third condition ascribes authority to the results of external monitoring over self-monitoring and thereby pre-empts the use of self-monitoring as a means of questioning the former.

Inasmuch as the APU aspires to impose these kinds of limits on the development of self-evaluation methods in schools it can only be considered to be a constraint both on the professional autonomy of teachers with respect to the question of their responsibilities towards pupils and on the emergence of genuine dialogue between teachers, schools and the general public about the nature of those responsibilities.

Accountability: An Alternative Model

However, it is possible to produce a form of public accountability which both respects the professional autonomy of teachers and their right to dialogue with the public about their responsibilities. Its main features would be as follows:

1. A school and its teachers would acknowledge accountability to their public by producing their own self-evaluation reports for public scrutiny and discussion. As a check against bias they could incorporate discussion with external evaluation consultants who had free access to classrooms and the school.
2. A school and its teachers would self-evaluate in the light of their own conceptions of the sort of things they are accountable for, but the evaluation reports should make these criteria clear and indicate a willingness to enter into dialogue with their public about them. Such an indication might involve incorporating into reports, questions and issues about the criteria which are raised by the external evaluation consultants.

3. A school and its teachers would accept responsibility for establishing contexts in which genuine discussion and dialogue could take place and procedures for formulating and adapting policy as a result.

Such procedures would ground public accountability in dialogue, and in doing so reconcile the obligation of schools and teachers to be responsive to public opinion with their professional autonomy. They define quite a different conception of accountability to the one now emerging at the political/administrative level, which are basically methods of bureaucratic control. It is too much to expect central and local administrative systems to encourage the growth of what Ernie House has called 'responsible accountability' which is grounded in dialogue and based on the development of the self-monitoring capacity of schools and teachers. The initiative for developing and sustaining this alternative model must come from the teaching profession and the schools. If the challenge is neglected then teachers will deserve to be treated as technicians and social engineers whose sphere of action is restricted to means rather than ends, rather than as professionals who are allowed to self-determine their own ends. It will also, of course, mean 'the demise of dialogue' amongst teachers about fundamental educational issues.

Self-evaluation for Progressive Education

Finally, I want to explore the sort of self-evaluation it is appropriate for progressive teachers to engage in, if their major aim is to promote rational autonomy on the part of their pupils. I believe their aim of rational autonomy is better conceived in terms of promoting particular educational processes than in producing particular measurable results. It is possible through logical analysis of the aim to specify what teachers have to do to provide pupils with opportunities for autonomous learning.

Work with teachers on the Ford T project produced the following procedural principles:

Negative Principles

The teacher should:

1. Refrain from preventing pupils from identifying and initiating their own problems for investigation.
2. Refrain from preventing pupils from expressing their own ideas and hypotheses.
3. Refrain from restricting students' access to relevant evidence and drawing their own conclusions from it.
4. Refrain from restricting students' access to discussion.

Positive Principles

The teacher should:

1. Help students to develop the capacity to identify and initiate their own problems.
2. Help students to develop their own ideas into testable hypotheses.
3. Help students to evaluate evidence in the light of its relevance, truth and sufficiency.
4. Help students to learn how to discuss.

Conformity tc such procedural criteria as those listed above does not so much ensure that pupils will learn autonomously as ensure the conditions in their learning environment which give them adequate opportunity to do so. It is important to stress that one cannot make pupils learn autonomously as one can often make them learn to believe or do certain things.

I would suggest that however intuitive progressive teachers' conceptions of their responsibilities are, the kinds of procedural criteria I have cited come nearer to reflecting them than the achievement criteria specified by bureaucratically-controlled monitoring systems. They specify the sort of things progressive teachers and schools would use, albeit intuitively, as a basis for self-evaluation. Self-evaluation against such process criteria requires teachers and schools to assess the extent to which the means specified by their aim have been implemented rather than to assess the causal relationship between means and intended learning outcomes. In my view, much of what passes for progressive education in our schools is only superficially so, and I believe that more self-evaluation at the implementation level would reveal how far progressives have to go in translating their ideals into practice.

Some will argue that public accounting procedures based on self-conducted case studies of the quality of the intellectual climate in classrooms is hardly going to appeal to a public which evaluates education in terms of its results. But it is a mistake to equate what the public thinks is in its interest and what is in fact in its interest. In the context of dialogue I believe it possible for progressive teachers to put forward good reasons why making provision for the development of rational autonomy in schools is in the public interest. I haven't space to clarify these reasons in depth but they would be related to the fact that a society cannot survive as a democracy without citizens who have developed the capacity to self-determine their own beliefs and conduct.

References

Ennis, R. (1973) 'On causality' *Educational Researcher* 2(6).

Kay, B. (1976) 'The assessment of performance unit: Its task and rationale' *Education 3-13*, 4(2).

Jackson, P. (1968) *Life in Classrooms* New York, Holt, Rinehart and Winston.

Start, K. (1974) 'Establishing children's learning as the criterion for teacher effectiveness' *Educational Research* 16(3).

4
Matching and Evaluation

The Plowden Report contained many thought-provoking passages, but one stands out as capturing most succinctly what is of import and challenge to all concerned with children's learning:

> 'Learning is a continuous process from birth. The teacher's task is to provide an environment and opportunities which are sufficiently challenging for children and yet not so difficult as to be outside their reach. There has to be the right mixture of the familiar and the novel, the right match to the stage of learning the child has reached. If the material is too familiar or the learning skills too easy, children will become inattentive and bored. If too great maturity is demanded of them, they fall back on half remembered formulae and become concerned only to give the reply the teacher wants. Children can think and form concepts, so long as they work at their own level, and are not made to feel that they are failures.'
>
> Para, 533 (CAGE, 1967)

The concept of 'match' was taken as one important theme in the HMI survey of primary schools, where an attempt was made to quantify the 'degree of match' for children in different ability groups within their class in various subject areas. These data provide, at last, some measure (however crude) of how well matching is carried out in schools. For some areas of the curriculum, notably science and the humanities, the findings are not happy ones. But they are not surprising to anyone who is closely involved in primary education, and they cannot be easily dismissed. Arguments have been advanced that matching is not important, indeed that learning can take place better when there is 'mismatching' (Bennett, 1978), but I believe such arguments suggest a difference of interpretation of matching rather than a serious disclaimer of matching as proposed here. It is clearly important to discuss just what we do mean by matching and the part it plays in helping learning. Firstly, however, we take a more detailed look at the findings in the HMI survey about matching.

Table 1. Classes achieving reasonably satisfactory match for less able groups

	Less able groups		
Percentage of classes	7-year old classes	9-year old classes	11-year old classes
94-85	Reading	Reading	Reading
84-75	Mathematics Writing Spoken language Physical education	Mathematics Writing	Mathematics Writing
74-65	Music	Spoken language Physical education Music	Spoken language Physical education History
65-55	Art and Craft	History	Music Geography

54-45	History Geography	Geography	Art and Craft
44-35	Science (observational) Science (experimental)	Art and Craft Science (observational)	Science (observational) Science (experimental)
34-25	–	Science (experimental)	–

Table 2. Classes achieving reasonably match for the average groups

	Average groups		
Percentage of classes	7-year old classes	9-year old classes	11-year old classes
94-85	Reading	Reading	–
84-75	Mathematics	Mathematics	Reading Mathematics
74-65	Physical education Writing Spoken language Music	Physical education Writing	Physical education Writing Spoken language
64-55	–	Spoken language Music	Music History
54-45	History Art and Craft	History	Geography
44-35	Geography Science (observational)	Geography Art and Craft	Art and craft Science (observational)
34-25	Science (experimental)	Science (observational)	Science (experimental)
24-20	–	Science (experimental)	–

Table 3. Classes achieving reasonably satisfactory match for more able groups

	More able groups		
Percentage of classes	7-year old classes	9-year old classes	11-year old classes
64-55	Reading Physical education Spoken language	Reading Physical education	Reading Physical education
54-45	Mathematics Music Writing	Mathematics Music	Mathematics Music Spoken language
44-35	Art and Craft	Writing Spoken language	Writing
34-25	History Geography	–	Art and Craft History
24-15	Science (observational) Science (experimental)	Art and Craft History Geography Science (observational)	Geography Science (observa-tional) Science (experi-mental)
14-10	–	Science (experimental)	—

To appreciate the full weight of the survey results about matching it is necessary to look at all the three tables for less able, average and more able groups, each at three age levels (Tables 1-3). The judgment as to ability level was made by the teachers and this part of the method of gathering the data has been criticized. These criticisms do not, however, weaken the force of these results, for what happens in a classroom that affects matching depends on the teacher's views of the ability of individual pupils, not on a more objective measure of ability not known to the teacher. The striking patterns in these results hardly need to be pointed out. It is clear that the order of success in matching among different subjects varies little, with reading, mathematics, writing and physical education being consistently near the top of the scale. At the bottom, with heavy constancy, is science, with geography and history, art and craft not far ahead. It is also clear that the proportion of good match improves from the more able to the average to the less able and, to a smaller extent, from older to younger pupils.

Interpretations

How can we interpret these findings? As a concerned science educationist I might put the question more pointedly: why is science always at the bottom of the pile, not only in matching, but also, as is clear elsewhere in the report (chapter 5 iv) in the provision of adequate time and equipment? There is something more important at stake here, though, than just the interest of one subject area and the question has to be discussed in more general terms. The survey itself confirmed what many teachers would like to believe, that 'the range of work and the standards achieved are related, sometimes in ways that are not immediately obvious; for example, a narrow concentration on teaching a skill is not always the best way of achieving high standards in it' (6.1). The inclusion of a range of subjects beyond the 'basics' is thus seen to be not only worthwhile for development in these subjects but also for the 'basics' themselves. However, it is in the subjects 'beyond the basics', the art, the humanities, the sciences, that 'matching' is least apparent. Thus we return to the question of how this comes about.

There are several possible factors which might well be associated, though no one could be described as the cause. First, the order of descending success in matching is also the order of descending 'importance' of subjects, as seen in most people's eyes. This is a fact which is largely common knowledge, but also has the support of research. The project on 'The Aims of Primary Education' reported that the results of teachers' ratings of different aims were that 'conspicuous by their complete absence among the priority aims were any references to the arts, music, physical education,' religious education, sex education, science or a second language. Aims in all of these areas were congregated in the lower half of the rank order and most of them failed to reach even an average rank of "important"' (Ashton *et al*, 1975, p. 62). We may regret that the notion of what is basic, and therefore important, in primary education does not extend to the concepts which help children understand the physical, human and social world around them, but it cannot be denied that this is the case at present. Also, it will take a great deal of time for any change in the established priorities. Putting this together with the 'matching' findings might suggest that what teachers do not consider important they do not teach very well. But it is too early to draw such conclusions, for there are other factors to be considered.

The second factor which may be associated with success in matching is a reflection of what is important in initial training programmes. Teachers cannot be expected to teach subjects well if their preparation in these subjects has been insufficient. Again it does not need any suspension of credibility to accept that the order of success in matching correlates with the order of time spent in training in the various subject areas. The peculiar difference which exists in some cases between what teachers are expected to do when in service and what their training covers is hard to understand. For example, the primary survey, whilst endorsing the use of posts of responsibility to provide a teacher with knowledge and ability to give leadership in planning and guiding work, did not advocate specialist teaching. In schools, each teacher is expected, with some help, to be able to deal with science, history, geography, and so on, yet there is a significant proportion of teachers leaving initial training courses without any training in teaching science and in at least one of the humanities.

A third factor might well be teachers' own background knowledge. In science this must certainly be very significant and could be no less important for history, geography, art and craft. At the primary level it is not important for pupils to learn about particular periods in history, particular facts in science, and so on, but rather to begin to develop concepts and study skills which can be applied to a range of subject-matter. However, to do this it is necessary for there to be *some* content to study, one does not learn to observe without observing *something*, or to reason logically without reasoning about *something*, or about how living things behave without studying some particular living things. A lack of knowledge of relevant facts, even though these do not have to be transmitted to the children, is undoubtedly inhibiting to a teacher. In science, particularly, we then have a situation leading to a vicious circle — of pupils having no adequate science experiences in the primary school, being deterred by academic science courses in the secondary school and leaving with a dislike of the subject, some to become teachers who perpetuate these conditions.

A fourth factor relates to the kind of materials which teachers have to help them. At the top end of the matching ratings we find reading and mathematics, for which ready worked out teaching schemes and materials abound. If he or she so wishes a teacher can use sets of books, for pupils and teacher, and associated aids which, on account of their structure, ensure a fair basis for matching. Such materials can never replace the sensitive interaction of teachers with pupils which is necessary for matching, but they at least provide the essential resources. As we go down the matching scale the degree of structure in materials recently produced for teachers declines. This is inevitable since these are subjects where complex concepts and sophisticated study skills are the aim, rather than mastery of a well-defined set of facts and procedures. Structure of the same kind as in reading schemes is thus not appropriate, but structure of a different kind is appropriate. It could be such as to indicate the development of various concepts in children and exemplify subject-matter which would foster it. Instead of this, much material for teachers tends to suggest isolated activities or topics which are not obviously related to the systematic development of underlying concepts and skills.

There may well be other factors which could be postulated as correlating with success in matching; it is likely to be a combination of factors, those mentioned and others, which accounts for differential success in matching. We can come a little nearer to finding the most likely causes by looking now at what is the meaning of matching, what it entails and why it is important. Support for its importance comes not only from the opinions of experienced educationists, as represented in the paragraph quoted above from the Plowden Report, but also from the findings of those who have studied children's mental development, for example Bruner (1960) and Piaget (1970), who may disagree on other matters but are of one voice in regard to matching. From a different angle again Bloom (1971) has pointed out the damaging consequences of mismatching.

The Meaning of Matching

Perhaps the first point to make about matching is that it does *not* mean giving children more of what they can already do. It is this misuse of the term which I believe is responsible for claims that learning is better when there is mismatching. What matching does mean, in simple terms, is finding out what children can already do and what ideas they have, as a basis for providing experiences which will develop these skills and concepts. The keynote of matching is thus finding the right challenge for a child, the size of step that he can take by using but also extending existing ideas. There is as much a mismatch if this step is too small, leading to boredom, as there is if it is too large, leading to failure.

The second point is to recognize that while this may seem reasonable and indeed obvious in theory, it is extremely difficult to translate into practice. The process of learning is dynamic, not static, and 'what children can do' is changing constantly. Furthermore, even if the difficulty of matching could be overcome for one child, the teacher has the problem of attempting this for thirty or more individuals, all varying in past experience, background and existing ideas. A child who can work at a more advanced level will be underoccupied by activities which provide a worthwhile challenge for another. The teacher has thus not only to attempt to cater for a multitude of differences between pupils but also to distinguish easy success, accompanied by signs of boredom and lack of interest, from success which results from a challenge which has made a pupil try hard and has resulted in some development in his thinking.

As if these complexities were not enough, we have further to acknowledge that it is not just the intellectual demand of an activity which has to be matched to the level from which the pupils can operate, but that there are other features of learners and learning experiences which have to be matched as well as possible. Past experiences and knowledge gained out of school interact with school activities, so that children will react differently to them. We find an obvious example of this in children's reactions to swimming classes at school; generally, reactions range from over-enthusiasm to cowering resistance. These reactions are physical and thus clearly observable, but there must be the same range of less observable reactions to the sight of the maths book or the sound of the word 'project'. In addition there are, of course, individual differences in interests, attitudes, preferred modes of learning and time required for particular activities.

All this might seem to suggest that hope has to be abandoned of putting into practice the idea of matching. But what it points to is that a solution in terms of a prescription or a set of guidelines cannot be expected. There is, however, strategy which can be adopted for improving the degree of matching, whilst it has to be admitted that the theoretical ideal of complete matching for every pupil all the time is unattainable. In teaching, decisions are all the time being made, to adapt or adjust materials, methods, organization pupil—pupil and pupil-teacher interactions. The aim of these decisions is to help the children's learning and it is through examining how these decisions are made that we can see how matching can be improved.

Figure 1 (after Harlen, 1978) looks at the decisions the teacher makes and the influences on such decision-making. Here the teacher, subject to external constraints and other influences, including his or her own ability, which limit the range of options, makes decisions about the learning environment and the intended outcomes. The phrase 'learning environment' is used here to convey the whole set of conditions arising from decisions about materials, methods, the teacher's role, etc., which affect the pupils' learning. The interaction of pupils and learning environment changes them both; the changes in the pupils may be both intended and unintended. There would be nothing wrong with this scheme of decision-making if we knew exactly how to bring about intended learning. But this is not the case for, as already mentioned, there are many factors influencing learning which make each situation unique. To take them into account the teacher needs more information as a basis for decisions than is suggested in the diagram. Since there are no prescriptions to be found for matching to every different set of circumstances, it is necessary to do this by a series of adjustments made in response to information about what is happening. Information is needed about pupils' ideas and about interactions of pupils with the learning environment so that the moment-to-moment decisions can respond to what is taking place. Instead of suggesting the teacher makes decisions independently of the response of the pupils, the model of decision-making for matching must show feedback being gathered and used, as illustrated in Fig. 2.

Here the dotted lines represent information gathered about the interaction of pupils and learning environment, about the pupils and about the outcomes, both intended and unintended. What cannot be easily represented in a diagram is that this process is a cyclic one. Information on its own does not solve the crucial problem of matching which concerns deciding the next step which each pupil can and should take. But if the process of making a decision and gathering information about its effect is a cyclic one, then the optimum conditions can be approached through a series of approximations. The effect of gathering information in this way is also cumulative, helping not only the present situation but building up a store of knowledge about pupils and activities which can inform future decisions. Thus this concept of matching is as a dynamic process in which feedback plays an essential role.

Figure 1. Influences and Feedback on Teacher Decision-Making

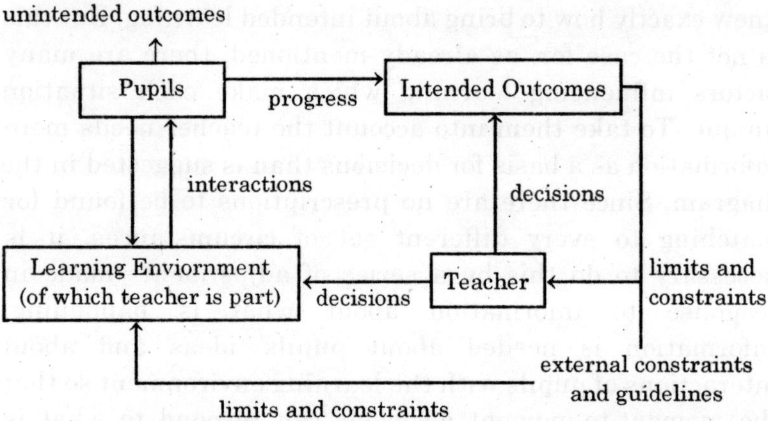

Most teachers will, hopefully, recognize this as something they already do, or attempt to do, but would not have found it necessary to analyze in this way. Analysis is necessary, however, if we wish to identify what kind of help teachers may need for matching to be improved. Teachers are required to make decisions about intended outcomes and so must be able to find help as to what lines of development are appropriate and what the points of this development are. This includes knowing, for example, that some ideas children will form would be described as 'wrong' by adult specialists, but are unavoidable steps in development because of children's limited experience and their ways of thinking. Having some idea of lines of progress which can be expected has to be supported by knowing how to foster progress; what methods, materials, activities are likely to be appropriate at each stage.

It has been stressed all along in this chapter that decisions about content are only part of the matter; methods and organizations are also important in providing learning opportunities. For too long the impression has been given that a single method and one type of organization is the answer to all teaching problems. 'Discovery learning' and 'informal' organization have been mistakenly advocated in this way at one time or another, as if they were panacea for teaching all parts of every subject. What teachers need to have is a repertoire of methods and organizations, but most important, to know how to select the appropriate ones for particular circumstances.

Opportunities to Improve the Gathering of Relevant Information

Basic to the attempt at matching is the gathering of feedback for the evaluation of what is happening and how pupils are responding. The word 'evaluation' is used advisedly here, instead of 'assessment' and it is relevant to explain the reason. Evaluation is a broad term which describes the collection of information and the clarification of criteria used in judging and using the information. Assessment describes a range of methods which can be used for collecting information. Assessment implies some attempt to measure or to compare with a standard, but this need not be a fixed and widely used standard. Thus a remark made to a child such as 'good', either spoken or written, implies an assessment, often in terms of a standard which applies only to that child. A similar response by another child might bring forth a different remark, since the assessment might be against a different set of expectations for that pupil. The word assessment covers a range of methods, from the use of standardized tests to informal observation using child-based standards, as just mentioned.

But there are other methods of gathering information than assessment. These others do not imply an attempt to summarize or measure; they can be best described as 'collection' or 'description'.

Figure 2. Influences and Feedback on Teacher Decision-Making

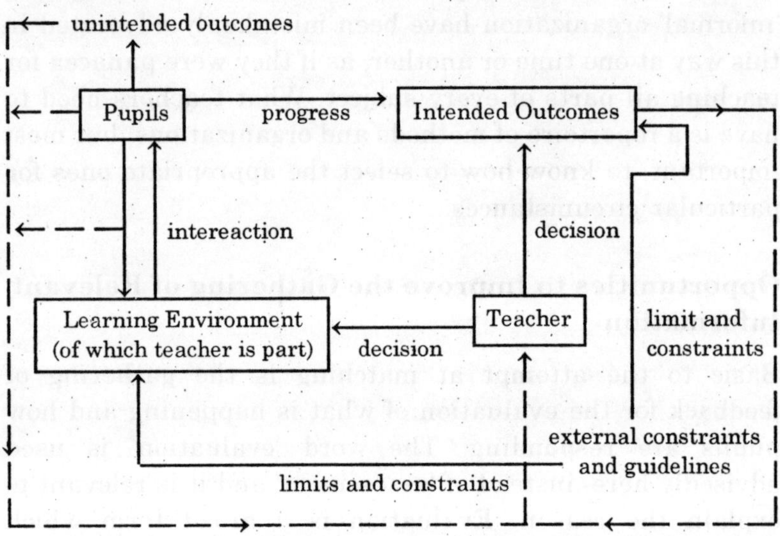

Taking samples of work, making notes describing behaviour, using recording techniques, are examples of these ways of gathering information. They do, of course, imply some selection on the part of the teacher and are often criticized as being too subjective for this reason. But it has to be remembered that all information is subjective to some degree. Even in objectively-marked standardized tests someone has decided what questions to ask, which abilities and facts will be covered and which left out. Subjectivity is inherent in all data gathering; it can be minimized if this is necessary, but there is a price to pay for it. It is very important for teachers to know when different methods are acceptable and when they are not. For just as in the case of selecting materials and methods for teaching, methods of evaluating have to be chosen to suit their purpose.

Although gathering information for matching serves quite a different purpose than assessment of pupils for determining local or national performance levels, it may be that the current interest in national or local assessment can be turned to advantage for helping the teaching-learning process. It is essential, however, to distinguish between the kinds of information required for these different purposes and to identify methods which are most suitable for each. The feedback which a teacher requires to help matching has to be gathered frequently and repeatedly, and must cover the whole range of teaching intentions - skills, attitudes, concepts. Methods used, therefore have to be unobtrusive and flexible so that information can be gathered about individual pupils at different times as required. Clearly they must not be time-consuming or demand special equipment or preparation, they must not interfere with learning activities, not disturb pupils or make them anxious; but they must still be as valid and reliable as possible. It is evident that testing of any kind does not meet these specifications. Tests have a role where comparisons are being made between pupils and it is important to control the kind of behaviour which is assessed. But what is required for matching is information about how the pupils are coping with their normal learning activities, not how they perform in specially contrived test situations.

Observation of pupils during their normal work is a method of gathering feedback which suits the requirements very well. Pupils are unaware of it taking place, it can be used as often as necessary, does not interfere with on-going work and will give information about all those aspects of development for which learning opportunities are provided. There are, of course, some disadvantages and hidden demands on the teacher. For whilst observation may not require preparation of materials, as testing does, it does require mental preparation in thinking out what to look for, in deciding criteria to be applied and in interpreting what is found. Moreover, since observation means more than looking, but involves a greater emphasis on listening and giving attention to certain of children's responses, it may well affect teaching style, so that more time can be spent in receiving signals and giving pupils more chance to explain their ideas and ways of thinking about things. Further discussion and examples of methods based on observation and of other methods for gathering information from pupils can be found in Harlen (1978).

It is also possible to turn the growing demands for accountability in education to advantage providing, that is, that schools maintain the initiative in this matter. The absence of pressure from outside for teachers to account for what they do has led, in some cases, to an absence of effort inside to evaluate what is done. A teacher has to be able to account to himself before he can account to others and this means extending the gathering of information beyond the bounds of the classroom to the functioning of the whole school. The feedback needed for matching can then be seen as part of a programme in which teachers and schools monitor themselves and constantly assess their success in providing a truly educational environment suited to their pupils. Accountability can be a positive and helpful force where it starts in the school, involves teachers in the clarification of their intentions and the evaluation of how well these are implemented and leads to a dialogue with those outside the school who have the right to know what is happening. The negative effect on schools of accountability schemes comes when these are imposed from outside the schools, applying criteria which may not be shared by those inside. The 'back to basics' move had many contributing factors but one was certainly that schools were caught unable to give good answers to why a broad curriculum was better than a narrow one.

Responding to New Demands — Some Issues

These are only some of the directions from which there appear to be forces combining to emphasize the importance in teachers' work of evaluation and self-appraisal. The possibility of teachers being able to respond to more demands depends, however, on two crucial conditions; that time is made available and that teachers receive the help to acquire or sharpen the necessary skills. It is no use disguising that evaluation is time-consuming, particularly when first undertaken. Evaluation can also save time by enabling better informed decisions, but there has to be an initial outlay of effort before there is compensation for it. Similarly, there can be no denying that changes of attitude may well be needed; there is little point in gathering information unless there is the willingness to take note of it, to accept the criticism of existing practice which it often entails and to make changes.

What can be done to ease the problem of making time for the in-service courses that will be needed by some to acquire skills of evaluation, time for gathering information and, most important, time to reflect on it? The frustrating situation at present is that opportunities potentially exist, in falling rolls, to re-allocate a teacher's time. For economic reasons these opportunities are being missed and teachers have no chance to spend less of their working time in pupil contact. There seems little practical alternative at the moment to teachers spending some of their own time in reflection and discussion with colleagues. The educational reasons for this are put in strong words by Elliott (1979): 'A school that is reluctant to engage in an honest self-appraisal reveals a lack of genuine concern about the extent to which its policies are socially and educationally worthwhile. Elliott also points out what the alternative is, that if schools do not evaluate themselves then others will do so from outside with the consequent loss of autonomy: 'Externally imposed evaluation systems are essentially the means of getting schools to comply with policies decided elsewhere.'

For all decisions, from the moment-to-moment ones aimed at matching activities to pupils to the ones at the level of policy which decide the broad framework of pupils' experiences, information is required. The techniques for collecting data are not complex nor do they require the services of experts, but teachers do need to know about them and especially how to choose relevant and efficient ones for particular purposes. The question then arises as to what kind of in-service education can provide the necessary help? We have learned much that is relevant in answering this question from the attempts to introduce new curriculum materials. When teachers have been presented with new *products* and told how to use them, the result has often been little or no real change of the kind intended. When involved in the process of examining what is lacking in existing practice and developing ways of improving it, then the innovation has been more likely to be implemented. It is through involvement that the process of dissemination of new skills or materials reaches the point that Rudduck and Kelly (1976) described as 're-education'. When dissemination falls short of this point it fails to bring about real changes. Similarly, in disseminating the new skills necessary for evaluation it is not sufficient to communicate what techniques exist or to provide new ones, but rather to involve teachers in discussing the need for evaluation, analyzing real problems and seeing for themselves where certain techniques are appropriate. It was the experience of the 'Progress in Learning Science' project which attempted to help with the process of matching, that solutions produced by others were not seen as helpful by teachers unless the thinking which had gone into them was experienced at first hand (Harlen, 1977).

Finally, returning to the problem of helping with matching, it may be that there is help which is required in those curriculum areas where matching is less satisfactory over and above making time and in-service courses available. It may be that some of the other possible associated factors mentioned at the beginning of this chapter should be examined. Pre-service courses could themselves be evaluated to see if they provide an adequate preparation for the demands on teachers, including the skills required for self-appraisal and for decision-making at various levels. Not everything can be done at the pre-service stage, however, and the whole professional preparation and continued development of teachers would benefit from a thorough examination of what is best attempted in pre-service and what in in-service. The lack of co-ordination between these is a waste of scarce time at both stages.

Further, we might re-examine the kind of help given to teachers in the areas where their own knowledge is likely to be patchy at best. Curriculum developers have frowned upon the notion of 'structured' materials preferring, for good theoretical reasons, to leave the decision about selecting and sequencing activities to teachers. But there are different kinds of structure and not all lead to poor teaching. It is perhaps time to be more open-minded about the value of different kinds of materials. A degree of structure is helpful both to teachers and pupil, but what this degree is varies between individuals. More work is necessary to discover how best to give the amount of support which some teachers must have to function with confidence and yet at the same time also provide the flexibility for adaptation to their needs of individual pupils. All this is to acknowledge that teachers are individuals, as are pupils, and vary in the need of support Matching is as relevant in helping teachers as it is in helping children.

References

Ashton, P., Kneen, P., Davies, F. and Holly, B.J. (1975) *The Aims of Primary Education: A Study of Teachers' Opinions,* Schools Council Research Series, London, Macmillian Education.

Bennett, N. (1978) *'Surveyed from a shaky base' Times Educational Supplement,* November 3.

Bloom, B.S. (1971) 'Affective consequence of school achieved in BLOCK, J.H. (Ed) *Mastery learning,* New York: Holt. Rinehart and Wmston.

Bruner, J.S. (1960) *The Process of Education,* New York: Vintage.

Central Advisory Council for Education (1967) *Children and their Primary Schools,* London, HMSO.

Elliott, J. (1979) 'The case for school self-evaluation' *Forum* Autumn.

Harlen, W. (1977) 'A Stonger teacher role in curriculum development' *Journal of Curriculum Studies,* 9(1), May.

Harlen, W. (1978) 'Evaluation and individual pupils' in Harlen, W. (Ed) *Evaluation and the Teacher's Role,* Schools Council Research Series, London, Macmillan Education.

Piaget, J. (1970) *Science of Education and the Psychology of the Child,* London, Longman.

Rudduck, J. and Kelly, P.J. (1976) The Dissemination of Curriculum Development Slough, NFER (European trend reports in educational research).

5
The Primary Teacher

Teachers as Professionals

A problem facing many primary teachers is the indefiniteness of their job — its lack of clear aims and methodology, as well as its increasingly uncertain 'professional' nature at a time when external bodies are claiming a larger say in determining curriculum content. Until recently things were more clear-cut, at least for teachers leaving their colleges of education with a belief in 'progressive' education. On a 'progressive' view, as I am using the term, educational aims are not things to be imposed on a child from without, but implicit in his own nature: the teacher's job is to create the conditions which best enable each child's individuality to unfold harmoniously. This picture of the 'progressive' teacher is very familiar and I need not elaborate it. What I do wish to emphasize is that progressivism gives the primary teacher *status*, indeed a remarkably high status. It makes her the unquestioned expert on how children should develop. How could external bodies, whether in the shape of the state, LEAs, Taylor Committee governors or whatever, decide on aims and content? The only person who knows what these should be must be both an authority on the laws of child development, and an expert on applying these sensitively to particular cases, that is, the teacher-psychologist of the progressive tradition. How, too, could a teacher have doubts about her basic aims and methodology ? Once again, the theory leaves no room for worries like these. It sees the teacher as a confident professional, the supreme authority on all classroom matters.

This model of professionalism has received some hard knocks in recent years and in my view rightly so. One cannot find out what the aims of education should be from any amount of child observation or psychological theory. Empirical facts do not embody ethical values. The teacher-psychologist of the progressives' model is not and could never be an authority on the broad content and aims of primary education.

The assumption that teachers should have the right to determine aims is unsound. Whatever aims teachers adopt must surely be intended to have *some* influence on the kind of person a pupil grows up to be, and thereby, however minimally, on the kind of society in which he grows up. Since decisions about the kind of society we should have are political decisions, the choice of this set of educational aims rather than that rests basically on a political judgment. The crucial question is: why should teachers be empowered to make such judgments? If they had some special expertise, which the rest of us lack, on the nature of the Good Society, things might be different. But they have not. There are *no* experts on this topic. It is because there are none that democrats believe that political decisions cannot be imposed on people in the name of authority: each man is potentially in as good a position as any other to contribute to political decisions.

For reasons like this many have been advocating recently that the aims of education and the broad framework of school curricula should no longer be determined by teachers, as they have been *de facto*, but democratically, whether at local or at national level. This demand seems to hold within it another threat to the notion of the primary teacher as a professional. She has already lost her credentials as an autonomous teacher-psychologist; and now, if the broad framework within which she is working is to be determined by the electorate, she is apparently to be reduced to no more than a functionary, an obedient executive of political decisions taken elsewhere.

Many non-teachers would welcome such a large circumscription of her role, as has become evident in public reactions to Tyndale and in the Great Debate. I myself have argued elsewhere against the excessive freedom given to teachers in the British system and in favour of greater public control over aims and content. But I have never made it clear, either publicly or to myself, how far I would wish this reversal of policy to be taken. Is the primary teacher to become a 'mere functionary' or is there still a place for professional autonomy?

I shall take it as read, as 1 have in the past, that the teacher should be indeed an authority on what teaching methods and detailed content she should use in specific situations; only she is in a position to know how publicly prescribed content is to be accommodated to the particular abilities, motivations etc. of each of her pupils. The difficulty arises not so much here but over the general framework in which she is working.

Teachers as Civil Servants

Supporters of teacher autonomy sometimes speak disparagingly of teachers' 'being turned into civil servants' under a regime of public control, pointing to continental experience to show the very little scope teachers there have to make independent decisions on curricular matters. But perhaps we need to explore the concept of teacher as civil servant a little further. Civil servants in Britain operate at various levels of autonomy, from the tightly circumscribed work of a clerical officer to the very broad scope which, say, a Permanent Secretary has in interpreting government policy. I see no reason why, if teachers in Britain are to become a kind of civil servant, they will have to operate at the more restricted, rather than the less restricted, end of this continuum. Why cannot we reconceptualize the teacher (in our context the primary teacher) as a senior rather than a junior civil servant?

Now I do not want to get into disputes about the proper organization of the civil service, about whether we should have the kinds of grades we do have, and so on. Perhaps present hierarchies should be scrapped, I don't know. I am only interested in the senior civil servant — national or local — as providing a possible model of what the primary teacher might be under a system of democratic control. First, both jobs would presuppose an acceptance, at least for professional purposes, of a democratically-decided policy forming a framework for all they did. One has, of course, to write in the qualification 'at least for professional purposes' since senior civil servants might *not* accept government policy as private citizens. Perhaps the same could be true of teachers. Problems of conscience will arise, of course. I say rather more about these below. Secondly, for all their subjugation to political authority, senior civil servants do not tend to complain about their lack of freedom. On the contrary: as we have seen, they have considerable room for autonomous interpretation of whatever guidelines are laid down. Teachers could be in a similar position. One might imagine it being publicly laid down, for instance, that such and such areas of science be normally prescribed as minimum achievements for children of such and such an age: this could well leave individual teachers of science considerable scope in deciding the best routes, given their particular constraints and opportunities, to lead to this destination. (This is only, of course, an illustration, not a prescription).

It may strike some as bizarre to compare, say, the teachers of reception classes to senior civil servants. These teachers themselves may be the first to ridicule this idea: the gap between the two sorts of work, the status gap, if you like, is just too enormous. But how far do we think like this because we have conditioned ourselves over the years to do so? Other cultures, other thinkers have had a more exalted picture of the teacher than the British (or, rather, the English and Welsh, since the Scots have tended in another direction). It is true that there is one significant difference between teachers and senior civil servants, but this should not obscure the way in which they are alike. They are alike in that there need be no one between them and their political masters who 'interprets', as I have put it, political policy, that is, translates it into practical courses of action. In this way, teachers are different from, say, *clerical* civil servants, since the latter *do* have others above them who do this interpreting. The significant difference between teachers and senior civil servants is this: individual civil servants help to forge plans of action applying to the country (or county or borough etc.) as a whole, while individual teachers' translations of public policy apply only to the pupils they teach. No doubt this is one, and one well-founded, source of the ridicule which would meet the attempt to put the infant teacher and the senior civil servant under the same umbrella. But the difference here is only quantitative: *qualitatively* the two kinds of job may still be similar, in that they can both embody the 'interpreting' role described above.

Many would want to argue, even so, that the civil servant's job is immeasurably more *complex* than the primary teacher's and so cannot be fruitfully compared with it. But *is* it more complex? Think for a moment of the difficult judgments parents constantly have to make about just *one* child's moral development. This problem is compounded many times over for the teacher, even if she has a small class. Add to this the many-sided judgments she has to make about the selection and presentation of material across the whole curriculum, as well as the fact (quite alien to the civil servant's situation) that while making many of these decisions she is at the same time functioning as a model for the children of how they should behave and think — and it should be abundantly clear just how very complex her job is.

In some ways, of course, the jobs of teacher and civil servant are very different. For one thing, teachers do not have hierarchies of subordinates working beneath them. But this will not be seen as a disadvantage by any but the more megalomaniac of teachers. At least teachers need not be tempted into any of the various types of authoritarianism which may entice those at the top of bureaucratic trees. Some of them *can* be so tempted, if they choose to organize their school in a rigidly hierarchical way, but the smallness of scale of the institutions in which they work makes democratic regimes, perhaps even without heads, a possibility. For this reason, primary teachers often have better opportunities to create such regimes than their secondary colleagues. In general, horizontal relationships between equals could become the dominant kind of bonding in the teaching profession, without the vertical, superior-inferior relationships found in the civil service. The need for such horizontal links among teachers, as I am now conceiving them, should be obvious. Teachers of children of different ages cannot be left to interpret officially laid down guidelines completely independently: the teacher of six years old has some responsibility to see that what she teaches meshes in with what the teachers of the same children at ten, twelve or fourteen do with them. It is sometimes urged against the comparison between teachers and senior civil servants that the latter are small, close-knit bodies and that teachers can never hope to emulate them in their cohesiveness since they are so numerous and so scattered. But there is no reason why the teachers in different schools in the same local area should not dovetail their curricula and syllabuses, working as a single unit in much the same way as senior civil servants, with, for instance, far more mobility between different institutions in the system, There is, in fact, every reason why they should cooperate in this way; otherwise the education which any particular pupil will receive in the whole course of his schooling is likely to be the hit-and-miss, hotchpotch affair it too often is today.

I hope these various points are enough to show where I am laying the emphasis in the comparison between the primary teacher and the senior civil servant. Despite the several ways in which they are different, both of them are in the unique position of being the direct translators of political policy into more determinate courses of action.

Teachers as Reflective Thinkers

The new role I have been sketching for the primary teacher is very different from that in the progressive tradition. She will above all be a person of wide horizons. She will need, first, to understand the aims of the whole education system as democratically laid down; she will need to reflect on how to fit her own teaching into this framework ensuring at the same time that it meshes in with what her colleagues are doing in other institutions. Her horizons can no longer be bounded by her school, let alone, as with some of our most autonomous primary teachers today, by her classroom. She must see her day-to-day activity ultimately against the political framework which is to give it its *raison d'etre*.

I am aware that this conception of the primary teacher runs quite against everything that we have come to expect of her. Of all members of the teaching profession, she has traditionally been the least politically aware. Her typical milieu has been the world of art and crafts, of movement and drama, of learning to read and count. It has typically been a cosy, inward-looking world, quite cut off from the complexities of politics. The new primary teacher will need to be more knowledgeable, more reflective about society and its values than her present-day counterpart. It is difficult to draw a line round the kinds of knowledge one would ideally require of her. A deeper understanding of political realities necessitates some knowledge of economics, sociology, applied science, social and political history ... one could go on and on. A deeper reflectiveness about aims and their realization depends among other things on something of a philosophical understanding. All this imposes great intellectual demands on her, demands which her initial training can never hope to meet on its own, if at all I shall come back to this point later.

Meanwhile let me take up in more detail the point just made about reflection on aims. Ideally one would hope that public prescriptions about aims and content were also backed by a public rationale, which discussed in full such matters as the justification of different proposals and the relative priority to be given to each. Teachers will have to be able to argue their way around such rationalia.

If this kind of educational ideal is ever to be realised, it is clear that primary teachers will have to be far more adequately trained than hitherto to reflect on the larger purposes of their job. Their current lack of sophistication in this field, which emerges, as we shall see in a moment, from the Schools Council's *Aims into Practice in the Primary School* (Ashton *et al*, 1975), is not to be blamed on them. It is the product of a system in which discussion of aims has been, wittingly or unwittingly, discouraged, for fear of opening rifts between ideological positions and endangering a 'consensus' thought necessary for the system to operate.

A brief look at *Aims into Practice* will show more clearly the kind of reflectiveness required. The book is based on a survey of primary teachers' objectives. It discovered that their views on aims (I am using 'aim' and 'objective' interchangeably) tend to lie in a continuum. At one extreme teachers believe that 'education is the means used by society ... to ensure that new generations will maintain it both practically and ideologically' (p. 11). Such teachers 'rate as most important aims dealing the basic skills and with conventionally acceptable social behaviour' (p. 12). At the other extreme 'is the view that education is a personal service to the individual' (p. 11). Here the aims thought most important are 'concerned with developing independence, both emotional and intellectual, and with a much broader educational front, including art, music, movement, drama, and so on' (p. 12). Few teachers, we are told, are exclusively attached to one of these extreme positions: 'the great majority hold both to some extent' (p. 11), but with differing emphases.

The tension described is immediately recognizable. So, too, is the compromise which many teachers seem to settle for, that is, to pay a certain amount of attention to basic skills and in the rest of the time to foster the child's personal development by allowing him plenty of choice among *activities*, especially creative activities; a regime, for instance, of reading and sums in the morning, 'choosing time' in the afternoon.

The question now is: have those teachers — that is, most teachers — who adhere to both ends of the continuum really thought things through in depth? I am sceptical. For if one looks at all closely at either of the competitors, one sees obvious deficiencies. Why should the society-centred view, for example, put such emphasis on basic skills and conventionally acceptable social behaviour? Why not on the arts, on science, on political understanding? If we are concerned with the well-being of society, why should this broader understanding be thought less important? Presumably it is because the society-centred aim is dominated, as in the 'Great Debate', by economic demands: we will not survive as an industrial nation without a work force that is literate and numerate and also industrious, punctual and cooperative. But why should economic considerations be overriding? Citizens of a society are more than workers, and there is no reason why their education should be restricted in this way. Why, too, should the *status quo* be taken as a baseline? Perhaps 'conventionally acceptable social behaviour' is unacceptable from another, namely a moral, point of view. Just because conventional ways of doing things do exist or have existed, this is no reason for claiming that they should exist.

Narrowness of vision also affects the pupil-centred point of view. Why should creative activities in art, movement, music and drama etc. be especially highlighted? There are historical reasons for this, I believe, to do especially with, Percy Nunn's aesthetically-inclined theory of 'individuality'. If we are concerned with the well-being of the individual, why are science or political understanding (again) to be played down? Won't the pupil need *all sorts of* intellectual equipment, and not just the aesthetic, properly to fulfil himself?

But now we are getting into difficult waters. What is to

count as 'self-fulfilment' or as the 'well-being of the individual' is a philosophical problem of some depth. So, too, is the meaning of the 'well-being of society'. Whatever one finally says about both these matters, two things should be clear at the outset. First, there is no good reason to narrow them down in the way proposed. The compromise curriculum, of basic skills, social training and plenty of creative activities is too thin a diet. Second, the opposition of pupil to society is misconceived, simply because the pupil is a member of society. Of course, if 'social needs' are to be limited to the requirements of the industrial establishment, then the pupil may indeed have no part in this, except as a means to others' ends; and it is as a reaction to this that many teachers have taken up the cause of individual self-development. But if 'society' is to be understood in any less restrictive sense, which includes the pupil himself as one of its members, the whole continuum of aims on which *Aims into Practice* located so many of its teachers, simply collapses.

We would do well to abandon the continuum. It is rooted in conflicting attitudes to modern industrial society. Against those who see education as the handmaiden of industry are those unwilling to sacrifice individuals' potentialities to capital's demands. But their reaction is often too negative. It leads too readily to a fruitless escapism: if the 'real world' of industry is too inhuman to contemplate, let us turn our backs on it and paint and sing and do collages. Teachers who hold both attitudes — that is, the majority discovered by the survey — must be riven by conflict, half chained to necessity and half desiring to be free of it. It would not be surprising if this conflict were transmitted gradually to their pupils. And is this not indeed precisely what we find in a large part of our adult population today: on the one side a resignation to industrial semi-serfdom, and on the other the vain hope that one may one day strike it rich ?

The continuum merely mirrors the social *status quo*. It allows little or no place to any critical challenge to it. This comes out very clearly in the recent HMI survey of *Primary Education in England*. (HMI, 1978). This draws attention to the schools' general failure to teach pupils to argue a case, to reason things out. Social studies and science, both areas in which critical skills may be developed, are particularly ill provided for. (Political education is presumably so little in evidence in any of the schools surveyed that it is not mentioned even once).

This is not the place to go in detail into what should replace the continuum, assuming it is abandoned. But I have at least hinted at the need to see individual pupils as members of society, not as standing over against it; to reconsider how the 'good of society' and the 'good of the individual' are really to be opposed; to broaden the primary curriculum, whether approached from 'society' or from the 'individual'; to create a new kind of industrial society in which there is less escapism because there is less sense of servitude. This last remark, I believe, strikes at the heart of things. We need somehow to construct a society in which men can work without the thought that they are sacrificing their one, unique life for nothing; in which their work is freely and willingly undertaken as a condition of their own and others' self-fulfilment. How this will be possible without a wide-scale democratization of industry and a political education to prepare one for it, I do not know (see White, 1979).

Teachers as Political Activists

I have argued that *Aims into Practice* reveals that if the primary teacher's role is to be remodelled in the way described, she will have to reflect more deeply than at present on aims. She should not take for granted what passes as the conventional wisdom, but should follow through the logic of an argument to its underlying assumptions, challenge these assumptions, put forward less inadequate alternatives if the latter prove wanting. This will lead her inevitably to frame her own picture of the kind of society we should be working to create. If my intuition is correct, reason will guide her towards the vision of a participatory democracy in both industry and in local and national politics. Obviously more would need to be said in support of this view. But, if correct, it brings out the point that the kind of reflectiveness one may expect in a teacher about her aims is all of a piece with the reflectiveness one would look for in her as a citizen of a democracy: each role demands a sophisticated political awareness.

This comes out also in another way. As the person directly responsible for translating politically-determined aims into practice, she has some obligation to try to ensure that these official aims *are* so translatable. They may fail to be realizable in several ways: there may be practical difficulties in doing so; they may be impossibly vague or inconsistent; if one follows through their implications, they may be seen to be at odds with certain basic moral principles, and so on. Of these three kinds of defect specified, the first might make the aims *practically* unrealizable, the second *logically* unrealizable and the third *morally* unrealizable, that is, unrealizable by one whose basic moral principles they offended. So there is some obligation on the teacher, arising not only from her role as executant, but also from her being an autonomous moral agent, to bring pressure to bear to ensure that the official aims are aims that she can — practically, logically and morally — teach to. She is not to be a passive recipient of aims from above, but must play an active part in helping to improve them. This means political involvement — of two kinds. She has a duty to draw the attention of policy-makers to any practical or logical defects in actual guidelines. There must be *official* channels enabling her to do this. As for the moral obstacles, she can attempt to influence the political community — by pressure group activity, work within a political party, journalism or whatever — to change the guidelines themselves.

All this is implicit, I think, in the new model of the primary teacher. Not that every teacher will live up to all the expectations in the mode in every particular. Not all, for instance, despite what I seemed to say in the last paragraph, will be political activists. There is certainly, as I indicated, *some moral obligation* on them to be, if official aims are morally inadequate, in their view. But whether this obligation is to be overridden by other more important moral obligations is something that each individual teacher must be left to work out for herself. Certainly I do not mean to imply that the gifted teacher of music, who would be not nearly so good a teacher if she had to attend to political matters, should necessarily sacrifice her teaching. Whether she does so is a matter for own conscience. But at the very least, in *seeing* this as a matter for her own conscience, she must be aware of the conflicting obligations on her, the pedagogical and the political. And this means that she must possess the breadth of vision, the wide intellectual and moral horizons which I have been advocating.

Similar considerations apply to the teacher who has conscientious objections to official aims so great that she cannot teach to them. For her it is not a matter of accepting imperfect aims *pro tem*, trying meanwhile to improve them by political action : she just cannot in all conscience agree to them. For her, too, there will be a conflict of obligations, between accepting, on the one hand, that she is not arbitrarily to lay down her own aims, and being morally unable, on the other, to accept an actual democratically-arrived-at decision. For her, too, how she resolves the conflict — whether by bending the rules, by resignation, or however — must be left to her.

The Greatest Challenge

The new portrait of the primary teacher is so far from present actualities that many will dismiss it as impossibly utopian: it is too intellectually, perhaps even too spiritually, demanding for the average teacher; theoretically, it may form a pretty whole, but from a practical point of view it is a non-starter.

I disagree. What I hope to have done is set up some kind of signpost, indicating a new direction in which to move. How far we can get along the road I don't know. The greatest challenge is to find practical ways of getting the primary teacher to accept this grander conception of her role. Something, no doubt, may be attempted in her initial induction into the job of teaching during her pre-service training. But horizons cannot be widened at a stroke. Years of deepening understanding and reflectiveness are necessary, acquired in intimate association with practical classroom experience. How the teacher achieves this deepened understanding — by in-service courses, by informal discussion with colleagues, by solitary reflection — is another matter. It is a pity that our status-oriented society opens few paths before the ambitious young teacher beyond the climb up to headships, the inspectorate, LEA work or similar better-paid jobs. *No* work in education could be so responsible as the classroom teacher's and no work potentially so intellectually challenging. If we could once get the conditions of work right — manageable classes, adequate time to think out what one is doing, and so on —

what more 'successful' persons in the educational system could there be than the broad-visioned, practically competent classroom teacher?

References

Ashton, P., Keen, P., Davies, F. and Holly, B. (1975) *Aims into Practice in the Primary School*, London: University of London Press.

Her Majesty's Inspectorate (1978) *Primary Education in England*, London, HMSO.

White, P.A. (1979) 'Work-place democracy and political education', *Journal of Philosophy of Education* XIII.

6
The Politics of Primary Education

The number of live births in England and Wales in 1964 was 876,000. Since that date the number in each successive year has declined and the number of live births in 1977 was 569,000. Even if the slight upturn in the number of live births, which had occurred in the first three quarters of 1978, is maintained, the contraction of the primary school system, which has already been experienced for several years, is bound to continue, at least until the middle 1980s. This article looks at the implications of these facts for the education of children up to the age of thirteen under three broad headings. The first section deals with the major issues which arise, the second considers the factors affecting these issues and the third attempts to examine the decision — making processes through which those involved with the education service will deal with the issues.

Issues

The first set of issues concerns the organization of educational provision for children between the ages of three and thirteen. Clearly the decline in rolls, which is very unevenly distributed in different parts of England and Wales, is equally unevenly distributed as between different areas within an individual authority. The contraction of an individual primary school may eventually give rise to the question as to whether the school is still viable and whether, and if so at what stage, it should be closed. This is a highly politically sensitive issue and one which operates differently in urban areas where alternative primary schools are readily accessible as compared with rural areas where distances are different and where the relationship between a primary school and the area it serves is of a quite different character.

Over and above the critical issue of sheer survival, questions of organization and reorganization arise in a contracting situation. The most common of these are where there has been, during a period of expansion, an infants' and a junior school on the same site or at least serving the same immediate area. Decisions have to be made as to how long a separate infants' department in particular should remain a separate school in terms of the Burnham report and, in particular, in terms of separate headship. Educational arguments for and against the all-through five to eleven or five to twelve school ought to be considered more frequently and more radically in a contracting situation. There has, indeed, been a fairly general tendency to reorganize separate infants' and junior departments, roughly at the stage when there is no more than a single form of entry in each year. Other organizational changes have already affected the upper end of the primary school, with various authorities restructuring their provision on a pattern of first schools from five to eight, middle schools from eight to twelve and secondary schools taking in their pupils at twelve instead of eleven. The variant of the reconstruction of the secondary system to provide for middle schools, of course, directly affects the size and, therefore, the viability of the primary school. There have been areas where the reconstruction has given nine to thirteen schools, others ten to thirteen, still others eleven to fourteen. Policy changes by individual authorities to modify the former five to eleven,

eleven to sixteen or eleven to eighteen pattern for educational or other reasons have been, in a number of cases, overtaken by falling rolls which have introduced a new factor into consideration of the individual changes, so that many authorities find themselves at the present time with a heterogeneous pattern; The formation of the new local education authorities in 1974 has led, in many cases, to the amalgamation under one education committee of areas where different patterns had already been established. The extent to which the authorities have sought to bring about uniformity in the ages of transfer within the system across the whole of the area which they now cover has varied considerably and the stage reached in such further changes has varied even more widely.

A special aspect of the organization of education for young children has been the growth of nursery schools and nursery classes in the development introduced in 1972. The growth of pre-school education has again been extremely uneven, being most rapid in the inner city areas with the additional financial support provided for such development through a number of means and has been least in the rural areas of counties. Contraction in the primary schools has made accommodation available, so that much of the provision for children below the age of five has been in individual classes attached to and using accommodation in existing primary schools. Alongside this, however, and particularly in the first few years after the introduction of growth of nursery educational provision, there has been some development of separate nursery schools in the larger cities. A political educational issue at the present time, therefore, is the extent to which nursery education should continue to be expanded and whether or not this should be by the development of nursery classes in more and more individual primary schools, or by the establishment of further nursery schools.

The second major issue is that of staffing. Is the existing pupil/teacher ratio to be adhered to in a period of contraction or are the schools to be allowed to benefit from the retention of existing staff and to have a gradually improving pupil/teacher ratio ? Behind that broad policy issue lie a number of more detailed questions which very directly affect the individual school which is experiencing a fall in roll. Many authorities provide for a small pool of resources, often held at area or divisional level, which can be allocated at the discretion of officers or advisers to meet the particular circumstances of individual schools. Such circumstances are, of course, of a very varied nature—the proportion of immigrant or non-English speaking pupils, the degree of exceptional deprivation in the neighbourhood, all the factors which led to the setting up of the SP allowances with the recognition of the special problems of deprived areas. It is arguable that one of the circumstances to be taken into account in the allocation of a margin of additional help should be the difficulties which would be caused to the individual school by the strict application of the pupil/teacher ratio in a contracting situation. It is, in fact, in the 'small print' of the way in which an authority's overall ratio is applied to the individual school that the effect in the circumstances of contraction is generally felt. Let us take an oversimplified example. Suppose that the authority operates an overall pupil/teacher ratio for assistant staff (that is, excluding the head) of one to thirty. Then a six-class school with 180 pupils will neatly qualify for six teachers. At what point in the fall of the roll from 180 down to 150 is one of the six teachers withdrawn? Does the school have to reach 180 to get six teachers and to retain them? Or does the crunch line come at, say, 165? Or are the six teachers retained so long as the roll is over 150 ? There is all the difference in the way in which the school operates and in the average size of its classes according to the way in which the formula is applied. If the authority has taken a policy decision that no class need exceed thirty, then presumably at 151 on roll the school will retain its six teachers. This, however, is an unlikely situation and a more common one would be an intention that no class should exceed, say, thirty-five, the strict application of which would make it possible for the authority to withdraw one of the six teachers as soon as the roll fell to 175. This, however, would be unlikely and to a greater or lesser extent the issue then becomes one of judgment, presumably to be made by officers or advisers and to have a relationship to the use of the small pool of extra resources, if such exists, as to a satisfactory or at least not too unsatisfactory distribution of the children between the individual classes. The problem is one which is at its most acute in the summer term as the admissions of five plus children build up in January and again after Easter. In practice, most authorities make *ad hoc* and temporary arrangements if an extra class has to be created in the summer term but there is bound to be an annual, sometimes rather fraught discussion between heads and managers on the one side and the authority's administration on the other as to the number of classes to be established in the succeeding year in a contracting situation.

A further minor issue relating to staffing is whether the authority allows some of the pupils over and above the exact multiple of thirty, or whatever the basic ratio is, to be counted in such a way as to allow for the employment of part-time staff. Where the margins of extra resources are small, these are frequently distributed in terms of part-timers but, of course, the authority to employ such a teacher over and above, say, five teachers for one-hundred and sixty-five pupils against, a ratio of 1:30 would not be considered anything like as worthwhile as the ability to organize the school into six classes.

The other issue relating to staffing is the matter of redeployment, where the contracting school has to lose a teacher and where there is no resignation or retirement. Most authorities now have agreements with their teachers' associations at local level about redeployment arrangements and it seems as if these are working reasonably smoothly. For the individual teacher, redeployment may, on the one hand, be a moderately welcome opportunity for a change of scene or, on the other hand, an interruption of a desire for a continuity of teaching, often linked with a less acceptable journey. It seems as if the arrangements for the redeployment of individual teachers are being carried out with full consultation and with considerable care and many authorities show an acceptable degree of flexibility, insofar as they prove themselves prepared, if redeployment has not been satisfactorily arranged by the end of the school year, to leave the teacher at the existing school for a further period of time, till a satisfactory change can be arranged. The problem of longer journeys, particularly in county areas, is one which may or may not be met by the payment of additional travelling costs, which are in any case subject to income tax.

Two other matters relating to redeployment may be briefly mentioned: the first is that authorities have generally agreed with the teachers' associations that a teacher who has been redeployed should not be moved again for an agreed period. The length of that period seems to vary quite considerably from one authority to another. The second issue which arises occasionally is where it proves necessary to redeploy a teacher who is holding a post above the basic scale. This gives rise to a difficulty of the acceptability in the receiving school of a fresh teacher who will take up a scale 2 post which conceivably might have been allocated to an existing member of staff. Such an arrangement is likely to bring the managers into a greater or lesser degree of conflict with the administration and conceivably with the authority at political level. As far as the SP allowance is concerned, authorities will obviously seek to place a redeployed teacher from an SPA school in another SPA school, but where they have been unable to do this they appear to be overcoming the problem by a notional secondment of the teacher, retaining the SP allowance, to the non-SPA school, or by the offer to the teacher of a peripathetic scale 2 post as a recompense for the loss of the SP allowance.

The third issue and the one which, as far as the writer is aware, has been little investigated, is that of the curriculum. In the primary school, as distinct from the middle school, the almost universal arrangement for class teaching leads to the expectation that the curriculum in subject matter terms will be covered by each individual class teacher and the reduction in the number of classes, therefore, should not affect this matter. It is probably, however, not quite so simple as that. A particular example may well be that of music, where the school may enjoy the help of some visiting teachers or, more likely, will have a class teacher who is something of a music specialist and who will contribute to the musical education within the school as a whole. Should that teacher be the one who, for other reasons, has to be redeployed, then there may indeed be a significant effect on that particular aspect of the curriculum of the school. While music may be the simplest example, it would appear that some other subjects, such as science, possibly art or physical education, can suffer similarly by the loss of a particularly gifted teacher or one with some special contribution. It would be a matter of considerable interest if there could be carried out a series of studies of these rather hidden curricular changes in contracting primary schools.

At the level of the middle school, particularly where this is one that runs to thirteen or fourteen, some of the problems which are already being observed in the limited number of secondary schools which are experiencing falling rolls, may be expected to occur. The degree to which there is subject specialization in the middle school varies very widely and, of course, particularly with the differences in the upper age limit of such schools. In many cases, however, staff are appointed as specialists or semi-specialists and, given the relatively small size of most middle schools, some of the subjects have to be covered by no more than one specialist teacher. The contraction of such a school can lead to the situation where the staff must be reduced, and the most convenient way of such reduction is, of course, by natural wastage. This, however, may often operate in such a way as to remove from the school a teacher carrying, at any rate, some specialist teaching role and if there is to be no replacement, then that teaching must be spread among the remaining staff. Again, as far as one knows there is no specific information about this problem at this level, but it is undoubtedly an issue which will have to be considered in areas where the numbers in middle schools are already falling.

Finally, some reference may be made to the in-school organization of classes. In the primary sector, children are usually placed in classes according to age; there appears to be little streaming even in the junior sections of primary schools although it occurs, no doubt, in the middle schools. With the smaller primary schools, there has always been the need to have children of more than one year group in a particular class, and as the school contracts then this problem becomes more severe. The particular application of the staffing arrangements to the summer term roll will very much affect the need to move children from one class to another in the course of a school year, a practice which has always taken place but which is generally considered to be undesirable. It is unfortunately a practice which will probably be adopted increasingly in a period of contraction. There has in recent years, however, been a growth of family grouping arrangements as an approach to the organization of younger children into classes. Clearly a family grouping policy applied to the whole or a greater part of a primary school will tend to overcome difficulties of class grouping which arise where the intention is to place children in their year groups. It is important to recognize that family grouping has not been introduced to meet the problems of contraction, but equally important to observe that it is an arrangement which, in fact, does minimize those problems as far as class organization is concerned.

Major Factors

Let us consider now, and more briefly, the major factors affecting the issues which have been identified. The first of these is clearly finance. The education service within a local authority has to compete with the other local authority services for its share of the total resources and, of course, rate support grant is not ear-marked to individual services. Moreover the way in which rate support grant is distributed among the different authorities and notably between the urban areas on the one hand and the countries on the other means that the financial pressures upon the individual local education authority vary widely from one area to another. Be that as it may, there is always a ceiling on the amount of expenditure which the local authority is prepared to undertake from the rate support grant plus the rates themselves and thus upon the total expenditure on the education service. Such pressures tend to lead to an expectation that the real costs of the education service will be held at an existing level or not allowed to grow beyond a certain margin. They also tend to lead those who deal with finance to assume that the savings arising from a contraction of this or that part of the education service will, in fact, materialize — that is to say, an expectation that costs per head will remain similar. In a period of contraction, in fact, unit costs are bound to go up, since the fixed cost of maintaining an individual school is unchanged even though there are fewer pupils within it. Correspondingly, however, those concerned primarily with finance tend to expect that the other running costs, of which by far the largest is teaching staff, followed by non-teaching staff and including also capitation, will fall *pro rata* to the contraction in the roll.

The second factor is the judgment that has to be made about the viability of a particular school. Put bluntly, this means the judgment as to how small a school is allowed to become before it is closed. From the financial point of view, the smaller the school, the higher the cost per head, and the greater, therefore, the pressure at some stage to consider its closure, since that is a means by which the costs of the premises which cannot be changed can be taken out of the budget and, indeed, perhaps an opportunity to make other use of the building or even to realize its capital value. We are observing, at the present time, a mounting campaign to save village schools and any proposal to close a particular school, as we have observed earlier, raises a wide variety of issues and gives rise to many pressures. There is, however, a legitimate educational factor which is the professional judgment as to how small a school can be and still be regarded as educationally satisfactory. The answers given vary widely as does the judgment of successive Secretaries of State.

The third factor has been touched upon already, namely, that of the premises. This needs spelling out a little, however, if only to remark that the age and condition of the premises must be a fact to be taken into account, since these will affect the costs of maintenance quite significantly. The actual site of the school in question is also of very considerable importance, for in certain circumstances this may represent a very considerable capital asset, whereas in others its value either for other uses within the education service or for sale will be minimal.

The fourth factor to be taken into account is the broader social issue of the role of the particular school in the community it serves. This is especially the issue of the saving or closing of the village school, but the role of the school within the community, of whatever kind, is a factor of significance which ought to be taken into account as the roll contracts. A particular aspect of this factor is that the reduction of roll releases, or can release, accommodation which can be put to educational, or indeed other social purposes, within the community which the school continues to serve.

The final factor worth a reference is that of the operation of parental choice. In the urban circumstances of the great majority of the primary schools in this country, parents have some choice of school, in some cases a very considerable choice of school. Under conditions of pressure on accommodation, many authorities have operated fairly rigid catchment area arrangements for primary schools. As contraction takes place, these become less and less necessary and gradually fall out of use. In these circumstances, parents have a real choice of school and may well make this choice in response to their limited knowledge of this or that school and may well be affected by rumour, by influences of various kinds, including their attitude towards the proportion of non-white pupils in the school. The tale of the West Indian parent who refused to send his child to a particular school because there were too many black children there is by no means apocryphal. Given free parental choice, then, in a contracting situation, individual primary schools will undoubtedly contract at differing rates and the spectre of possible closure will approach more rapidly one school compared with another. If an authority intends to plan systematically the reduction in the number of its primary schools in an urban area, then it will at some stage presumably have to place limitations; once again, upon the operation of parental choice.

Decision-making

The last section of this article is concerned with decision — making about the issues in the light of the factors that have been identified. The general position is well-known, namely that powers of decision-making in the education service in this country are widely distributed and not, as in so many other countries, concentrated in a hierarchical pattern of authority. Those who have decision-making powers may be briefly listed: the Secretary of State and the Department of Education and Science; the local education authority acting at the level of the Council, the Education Committee, the subcommittees of the Education Committee, the Chairman of the committee or subcommittee or small sections set up *ad hoc* for particular purposes; the officers of the Authority; the advisers at the local authority level; the managers of the individual school; heads of schools; and the individual teachers themselves. A number of decisions are, in fact, reached as a result of the interplay of the powers and responsibilities of more than one of those listed.

In respect of organization and closure, some effective decision-making powers are exercised by parents themselves, insofar as by choosing one school and rejecting another, they are bringing about the contraction of a school to the point where reorganization from two departments to one department, or actual closure may eventually result. Decisions by the Education Committee or by officers as to the opening of nursery classes in one school rather than in another are likely to affect admissions to the primary school and competition to be allowed a nursery class may be a significant factor where the surplus of primary school places is inevitably going to lead to eventual closures. Admissions policy and, in particular, the detailed arrangements for catchment areas or for free parental choice are matters where decisions lie chiefly in the hands of administration. Heads, managers, teachers and parents all play a subtle part, however, in the whole process of admissions to one school rather than another, and press publicity at local or even at national level can, as experience has shown, affect the popularity or unpopularity of a particular school and, therefore, be influential (if not decisive) in matters of organization and closure.

The main decision-making power in respect of reorganization and of closure clearly lies with the local education authority and particularly with its schools' subcommittee. These bodies, however, act only upon the reports of officers who, in turn, will have been influenced, to a greater or lesser extent, by their professional advisers. The case for and against closure must be set out by the Chief Education Officer and his advice is clearly a major influence in the decision taken by the authority. If closure is proposed, that decision is, of course, a decision to issue Section 13 notices expressing an intention to close and the final power of approval lies with the Secretary of State. While at the primary school level party political factors are not of great importance in respect of individual decisions, there are factors of a political nature involved in the way in which the various people able to influence closure or not, in fact behave in particular circumstances. The key to the understanding of these matters is probably a recognition of the relative sensitiveness of the elected member to pressures brought to bear upon him by those who will have the opportunity of voting for or against him at a subsequent election. Indeed the timing of controversial proposals can be observed to have a significant relationship in many cases to the imminence or otherwise of local authority elections. The individually elected member is clearly more sensitive to pressures against the closure of a school in the area which he represents than he is to pressures from parents in other areas and probably the Chairman of the Education Committee and the Chairmen of the sub-committees are in a specially vulnerable position in this respect, though one is bound to say that it does not often appear to influence their own broad approach to their responsibilities for the service as a whole.

The factors affecting staffing have been referred to and the major one of these is cost. There is clearly likely to be continuing, very understandable pressure from the teachers' unions to improve staffing during a time of contraction, both on the educational grounds of the expected improvements from smaller classes and on the grounds that, with fewer children to educate, an authority can afford to retain teachers in such a way as to improve the pupil/teacher ratio. Critical decisions probably originate in the corporate management structure of the local authority and are taken, certainly as to overall staffing levels, in the group meeting of the controlling party of the authority in relation to the preparation of the budget. At this level of decision, the education service is very dependent upon the power and influence of the Chairman of the Education Committee and of other key members of what in many authorities is called a policy or a resources committee. Given that the local authority is one where there is a clear majority of one political party or the other, the influence of the party in opposition on this key matter of staffing numbers is probably minimal.

On the issue of redeployment, the broad policy is one where the teachers' unions have an important part to play and have clearly influenced the overall arrangements. The particular arrangements for the redeployment of the individual teacher seem to relate to decision-making powers by heads of schools and advisers or administrators at area or education office level. The identification of the teacher who is to be redeployed is a highly sensitive matter and seems to depend upon the interplay of the powers and advice of heads and advisers and administrators, with the teacher union representatives on the whole holding watching briefs rather than playing decisive parts.

Curriculum matters remain almost wholly within the hands of the heads and the teachers, but the impact of decisions about staffing, both as to overall numbers and as to redeployment, can be significant upon the details of the curricular provision. Managers, too, play a significant decision-making part in relation to employment of replacement teachers, though generally they follow the advice of the head of the school. It may be that managers will play some role in relation to the proposed loss of staff, not only as to numbers but in respect of the needs of the school. There probably are cases where the curriculum needs of the school would best be met by the retention of the most recently appointed teacher with some specialist ability to offer, and the redeployment of one who had been at the school rather longer. Where this is not readily acceptable to the teacher concerned, it may well be that managers might play a part in bringing pressure to bear in the interests of the maintenance of the curriculum. At primary level this is probably of very small importance but it is an aspect that may well become significant in individual cases at the middle school level where specialist teaching is more common.

Opportunity

Most of what has been said in this paper is about the problems of the primary school contraction. It is important to recognize the opportunities which that same contraction will give rise to. Fewer children in premises which, in the past, may well have been overcrowded will make it possible to provide more specialist areas, whether parts of larger rooms or whole rooms set aside for specialist purposes. It will release accommodation which can be used by other members of the community for educational activities and conceivably, therefore, can open up greater involvement between the school and its neighbourhood. Contraction ought, at any rate in the long term, to lead to staffing improvements and these should enhance the whole quality of primary education. The purpose of the whole provision of the education service, after all, is to provide the best possible learning experiences for the children concerned. It is probably not too optimistic to believe that, for the most part, those many people who have greater or less power of decision-making, in respect of the issues arising from contraction, will tend to consider the effect of this or that decision upon the quality of the education provided for the individual child. Judgments, however, upon many of the issues as to which decision is more likely to enhance the quality of education will continue to vary. The most critical, probably, is whether a very small school close at hand provides overall better educational opportunities than a considerably larger one some distance away. It is an issue which will be argued in many individual cases for a number of years yet.

7

Organization Development (OD) and the Primary School

Approaches

In recent years there has been an increasing interest in management ideas in education and quite a blossoming of courses of varying kinds and length. Many of these are concerned with technical and material aspects of management: the management of resources, educational planning and quantifiable aspects of education. Many teachers look first of all for practical and technical solutions but are usually disappointed when they come to apply the theories and techniques to their own schools. This is especially the situation for teachers and heads in small schools which do not seem to require 'heavy' management. Even in large schools it is quickly perceived that problems do not go away once a management technique has been applied; on the contrary, many management techniques only seem to make things more difficult and the pupils more remote.

In fact, the same problem has occurred in industry and commerce. Even when technological approaches to management have appeared to be relevant and to work, there has still been something important missing. The technical solutions have missed out on something organizationally essential — the sense of wholeness is the organization. People and the dynamics of people working together have been much more complex and much less open to 'managing' than has too often been presumed and, as a consequence, management theorists have begun to look harder at the nature of 'organization' and the ways organizations develop.

The term that has come into use to describe this organizational approach is Organization Development or 'OD'. Managers and consultants using OD approaches are concerned with the complexity of human dynamics in organizations and with helping people, managers and managed, to work out what is going on in the organization and to find out how to do things better, OD concentrates on the importance of mutual interaction, common responsibility, consensus, accountability and interdependence. A key feature in OD-based management is the use of consultants, both internal to the organization and brought in from outside, to help members sort out their problems and work through to new and mutually acceptable solutions.

OD is different from most other management approaches in that it is not confined to improving the quality of top and senior managers alone but is concerned to involve everyone in the organization in the management process. In practice, senior managers are often among the first to be trained in OD approaches but OD is not about teaching 'bosses' how to 'boss' but rather to help them to share management with their colleagues. Of late, an increasing number of heads have become interested in OD because of its concern with sharing and its helpfulness in understanding the dynamics of interpersonal relationships.

OD is not a familiar term in primary education management but, since its purpose is to interpret the things that have to be done to further the needs of the organization in terms of the needs of the people who have to do them, such an approach ought to appeal very much to teachers in primary schools. It is because primary school teachers have been concerned professionally with individual children as persons in their own right to be nurtured and encouraged creatively to explore their skills and talents and not as objects to be moulded and trained like artefacts, that so much that is worthwhile has happened in English education. And this is also a reason why humanistic approaches to management such as OD should have considerable appeal in primary education.

Organization Development: Some Assumptions and Concepts

The basic assumption in OD theory is that organizations are in their essential characteristics 'human' organizations and institutions. That is, they function in terms of people over and above any mechanical or technical considerations. Problems in organizations are seen not as mechanical problems but rather as problems of relationships among people. So unless problem-solving occurs in terms of people, the problems remain unsolved, however nicely mechanical and 'ideal' solutions may have been advanced. Schools are of particular interest as forms of organization because, like churches, they have no essential technology or mechanical quality that can obscure the ways people inter-relate. Schools are almost pure organizations in that they consist of people and nothing else of essential importance. A school may exist in a home, a palace, a field, a theatre, a church, or anywhere people can gather together and learn. But more than this, schools exist only because the activity of education exists, albeit in a formalized form. It is really the process of education that is organized, not the school; that is, the 'school' is an institutionalized form of education.

From the point of view of management theory (or, more correctly, organization theory, since theories of management derive from theories of organization) the essential factor in developing management strategies and skills is an understanding of the basic task (or mission) of the organization, and the critical relationship people have in the performance of that task. A common complaint about 'management theory' applied to education is that it ignores the child (or student). In fact, of course, this is only true of some mechanistic approaches to management. Proper theories of management such as OD acknowledge the true place of the child as central because the essential task of the school is the education of the child. Unless the school is organized around this basic task, the education of the child cannot properly take place.

But this is not to say that only the interests of the child are the concern of management. Organized education also involves teachers, parents and a variety of other people. All of these have legitimate needs and demands and they must be appropriately balanced against one another. It is usual for organization theorists to be concerned with the conflict of needs among children, teachers and others in the school. Clearly schools do not exist only for the children or only for the teachers, or the administrators, or the parents. Schools exist for all of them and their needs are by no means always compatible. There is considerable evidence, for instance, that the expressed wishes and needs of each group are in some measure incompatible with the wishes (and needs) of others. Schools 'work' only in sofaras these incompatible needs can be accommodated — not reconciled, not coalesced but allowed to exist alongside one another, a creative coexistence.

It must also be true that if there are significant differences between each major user group, there are also differences of a like order among each member of a group. It is quite nonsensical — as primary teachers know - to posit a complete identity of interest among all members of a group (be it a class of children, the whole child population or parents at large). Given that the school has no *essential* technology to influence behaviour, the inter-relationships among all the individuals who go to make up a school are exceedingly complex. The practical purpose of 'management' in its most usual manifestation is to reduce this complexity to simple and 'manageable' forms. Some people would argue that organization of such a complexity is so demanding that, in fact, essential purposes are overlooked and alternative, more manageable activities take place, so that the activities of the school become a kind of game, a pattern of ritualistic behaviour. This does happen, at least from time to time, and is one of the practical concerns management must deal with at some point, for it cannot be ignored for ever.

Because of the complexity of interests in the school, it is difficult to speak of goals and objectives as if there were an easy collective aggregation. By definition, organizational 'goals' cannot be individual goals also, so it is more appropriate in organization theory to talk of organizations as serving purposes; that is, they allow individual goals to be achieved through the group processes that occur within them. Some educationists write about institutional goal setting but a moment's thought will lead to the conclusion that this may well be no more than evasion of the issue of personalized needs. Though some American OD has concerned itself with collective goal setting, in the UK attention has been directed to helping people to understand just how individuals often use collectivity as a way of *avoiding* the personal dimensions of organizational activity.

Many people new to management ideas find the idea of 'structure' confusing. Older management texts talked of structure as if it were pre-existent, as if schools had inherent material structure. In fact, they have an exceedingly complex structure but it is not pre-existent. Structure is what actually occurs, not what one would like to occur. The structure of an organization derives from the activities the members choose to engage in, and these activities in turn are determined by the tasks members set themselves (albeit for a multiplicity of reasons). Functions derive from the performance of tasks and do not follow from positions with institutional tasks.

This is a difficult idea to explain. Organization theory describes behaviour as a 'function of the organization', hence any specific function (for example, learning, leadership) is primarily a function of the organization not the individual. Leadership behaviour is any behaviour that helps people to do their work: it may be performed by anyone in the group or organization and not necessarily the appointed leader. In this view, the heads of schools are not leaders by virtue of their position (that is, head) but only when doing whatever helps other members to perform the tasks, do their work. It is crucial to OD views of management to understand this; initiatives may come from anyone and are valid only in terms of their effectiveness, not the status of the person taking them.

This is a truly democratic view of organizations that is not acceptable to some people. Not only does it mean that all members of a school — teachers and children — are of equal functional status but it also means that they are equally responsible for what happens. It would appear that the concept of collective responsibility is often not well understood, particularly in large institutions. For example, collective responsibility does not mean that everyone should do everyone else's job, or that specialization is illegitimate. It does mean that no individual can say the responsibility for any action, decision or solution is not in some way their own, too. In a way, this is well understood in the infant school where the right of the children to make decisions and for the individual to choose what they want/need to do is accepted. A teacher cannot 'make' a child learn to read. They can only create conditions in which a child will exercise choices. Learning to make proper choices is at the core of education — learning rights and responsibilities. In the infant school, the pupil often has rights that are denied students in later stages of schooling, because infant schools are more child-centred.

Of course, in practice, educational institutions are run on a simplified pattern of predetermined role behaviour. But that does not mean that the underlying psychological conditions are changed. It cannot be said that when a head makes decisions which colleagues disagree with and the consequence is catastrophic that colleagues are therefore blameless if they did not attempt to influence the head otherwise. By and large people within organizations tend to leave decision-making to others and then complain when they do not like the consequences; they do not resist the original decision-making. Equally, heads who make bad decisions often complain that colleagues were not interested enough in the first place to offer advice and guidance. And some arrogant individuals take all the credit for good decisions but blame their colleagues for the bad ones.

Because organizations are complex psychological entities with a host of conflicting needs, interests and dispositions, all of which have in some way to coexist, they are arenas of active conflict. Some managers try to ignore this dynamic conflict, other refuse to admit its existence but the most effective managers use it to increase member involvement and commitment and so improve creativity and problem solving. In the past, OD has sometimes been accused of playing down conflict and stressing consensus-seeking but this is unfair, certainly within the English tradition. If conflict is inherent in all organizations, it would seem most sensible to use it rather than banish it. Because organization by its very nature is a limiting factor, members who are restrained from achieving their needs in some way or another become frustrated and alienated. But, if the reasons for alienation and frustration can be discovered, the creative forces in individuals can be channelled into positive organizational activity. OD is concerned to open up the dynamics of personal involvement in organizations and it does this by using skills of group facilitation and providing individual support, by helping members to accept and understand individual differences and the causes of conflict.

In summary, the theory of organizations that undergirds OD practice is that organizations are complexities of interpersonal relationships where individuals are motivated to participate only insofar as they see some personal advantage in so doing. Managing organizations by using OD skills means harnessing individual drives and the need for personal satisfactions so that the maximum number of members will feel their membership to be worthwhile and so put their effort into improving the quality of life in the organization. In this way the organization continues to provide necessary stimulus and reward until the members no longer have any use for that particular form of organization.

Change and Stress

It is important to grasp the idea that organizations, as means to ends, must necessarily be temporary. There is nothing in organization theory to suggest that organizations should continue for ever and certainly nothing to suggest that they should maintain the same form. Indeed, quite the contrary. It is a normal and reasonable expectation for organizations to be continually changing their form (structure) as needs, tasks, purposes and resources change — as they do continuously. It is remarkable how conservative people are about organizations though that is one of their characteristic dynamics. Good management holds the right relationship between change and conservation while nevertheless steering the organization through gentle and continuous change. And sometimes guiding it through cataclysmic and terrifying change, when circumstances so determine events. From the perspective of OD, change is of the essence of organizations but change must be made as benign as is humanly possible.

The degree of anxiety that organization itself creates, whether or not it is changing rapidly, is too often overlooked. Although organization can be supportive/ especially when it is self-determined, organization imposed from elsewhere is always a restraint and often a hurtful one. Because living in an organization means that one must overtly fulfil other people's expectation of oneself, organizations are stressful. Generally speaking, we understand this for children — and the good primary school attempts strenuously to mitigate the effect of expectations on individual children — but attention to staff is less forthcoming especially to senior staff such as heads.

OD is concerned to create a particular supportive and stimulating climate in the organization, a climate which is all pervasive. It is characterized by openness towards colleagues and a willingness to share, a preparedness to confront others when a concern is felt, a willingness to work through problems however difficult and uncomfortable, a readiness to accept responsibility and be committed to others, and a disposition towards being supportive and encouraging of colleagues. Because of the traditional role behaviour of heads, it is almost always essential for the head himself to be committed to OD and to be the first to be 'trained'. In this way, the person most vulnerable when the organizational changes consequent to OD occur is protected and he can support others through some of the crises that exploration of personal positions produces.

Much OD, at least in the early stages, is therapy of one sort or another. Organizations are themselves stressful situations but most people bring from outside anxieties, and concerns that affect their performance. Until these personal matters can be dealt with, no attention to the organization is of much consequence. Indeed, since organizations are only made up of individuals, ultimately the individual is the basic unit of concern. In my experience, OD without professional, personal help for members cannot achieve very much and may indeed only uncover deep-seated problems which are then incapable of resolution.

OD theory and practice have no room for cosmetic changes, because it is little more than cosmetic change that management conventionally attempts. It is no use attempting to change the structure without changing dispositions and attitudes and, of course, attitudes are dispositions most firmly held. The more entrenched attitudes have become, the more defensive they are and the more threatening appears the 'promise' to change them. By and large, OD practitioners prefer to work at the affective or emotional level of an individual or organization, believing that most attitudes are not susceptible to rational argument especially when there are critical problems in a conflict situation. That is not to say that people do not change attitudes and opinions rationally; they do. But, in the confusion of organizational situations, crisis or otherwise, people defend their beliefs because they feel the need to protect the public level of relationships.

An OD consultant does not, therefore, attempt to change attitudes head on but instead he creates situations in which attitudes can be examined and tested. He does this by creating experiential situations where trust can be tested and experienced, confidence can be built up and experiments in new relationships and behaviour successfully carried through. He is concerned to listen. He does not come with prepared answers or even packaged techniques. Any method can be used to share ideas — flip charts, pictures, montages, groups exercises and games. His objective is to help all members of the organization to listen and share before making decisions and then to work towards some agreement or acceptance of disagreement. Small groups meeting alone and then together, finding common ground and facing up to anxieties, fears and disagreements, are characteristic of the time spent in OD exercises. Formal meetings are conducted with openness and in a variety of modes rather than with tight authoritarian direction. This is not to say that OD, through a consultant, is undisciplined; the essential discipline comes from his deep understanding of group and organizational dynamics.

A consultant working in this way with a staff of a primary school will provide opportunities for individuals to present and discuss their feelings about the school, their hopes, concerns and misgivings. They will look at what they believe to be the needs of the children, the needs of the staff, their expectations of the head and how they would like to involve the parents and people from the education office. They will plan together and build a climate of common acceptance and mutual regard. An attempt will be made to help them to share what are the common problems and possible solutions will be discussed. At the end plans for action will be considered and some lines of action decided upon. The objective is to open up discussion and increase the level of participation and sense of involvement.

For OD to move on from this stage, training for the staff (or at least some of them) is essential. This training may take a variety of forms: counselling training, T-groups, encounter groups, workshops, problem-solving sessions. Particularly important is an understanding of group dynamics to facilitate the handling of meetings, committees and workshops. Once staff have been introduced to the skills involved, they can employ these in the normal working activities of the school. Such skills include listening, paraphrasing, sharing interpretations, suspending judgment, being supportive, confronting, levelling and so on. It is important that they occur in an open, supportive climate and are used in normal situations rather than being reserved for crises.

Consequences

Once under way, OD managerial approaches should increasingly result in improved skill in handling meetings, a willingness to confront one another over difficulties, a preparedness to resolve conflict, more use of personal counselling, third parties used as facilitators in problem areas, newer techniques for setting targets and an increased commitment to innovation, experiment and trying things out. Generally, the climate of the school should be easier, happier and there should be a greater readiness to take risks. People should really feel themselves to be partners and there should be a readiness to share problems and anxieties as well as hopes and dreams.

Perhaps it all sounds a little idealistic and that would be true. But the other side of OD is that it is often more realistic than other approaches to management just because there is less fear and a greater willingness to risk and explore because individuals better understand what really happens to people in organizations. Most organizations avoid upset and the deep issues: OD helps us to face them and resolve them.

One of the consequences of OD is that it demystifies management, making participants aware of the true place of technicalities and helping them to see that much of what goes on for management and administration is a cover for deeper failures and inadequacies. Once they begin to understand the true nature of organizations the latter begin to fall into their place and cease to be the giant, overpowering constructs we make them. My experience seems to confirm just how few people actually understand, let alone handle, what is going on in organizations, especially schools and colleges. The reason seems to have something to do with fear of intimacy, of closeness. To manage with people successfully you have to give something of yourself, to offer yourself, to expose yourself. You do not get close to people by parading your strengths, only by acknowledging publicly your vulnerabilities, your humanity. Too few managers can do this; they are afraid of their image slipping, their mask cracking, and that fear is what incapacitates them in their managerial behaviour.

I believe OD is more concerned to recognize the importance of learning, of coping with failure, and of recognizing our common humanity, than most other approaches to management. Organizations as we know them seem to want supermen, or even gods, to run them and so senior people try to exhibit these qualities. That is where they go wrong and why when they fall, they fall so far. Fear of failure is perhaps the most incapacitating mental condition that any person can experience yet organizations are so constructed that we dare not fail. It is not just that we create unrealistic levels of achievement but we pressure individuals to go well beyond what many can cope with. Yet we should learn the lesson of the good school where there is no such thing as failure but rather the acknowledgement that there are critical points of growth for individuals. The good primary school does not label children as failures, only as successes. Managers need to learn this, too.

But the practical consequence is that there is much deceit, pretence, and huffing and puffing in organizations, especially among senior members. OD can help them to come to terms with their true selves, show them that they are acceptable and good as they really are, if they will accept what they really are. Yet, strangely, to ask people to accept reality is often to receive the rebuff that it is unrealistic, impractical in the 'real' world. But the real world of most people is a desperate protective fantasy and it is the fantasy that is being protected. How can heads who fantasize about their schools be realistic about the pupils and *teachers*? As I hope I have shown, OD can help the shift to 'true reality' by its understanding of what organizations are and how people behave in them.

I hope I have shown that good management is a consequence of a clear understanding of what the organization is about. For the school that purpose is education, itself a process, not a content. An educated person is one who is continually growing up, maturing and learning, who can face the world with a disposition that will enable his experiences to work for him, an individual who grows in realistic confidence and personal awareness, who is unafraid of his inner self and fearless of others. It is a tall idealistic, philosophical order — a sense of continuity and searching but also of achievement and fulfilment. Schools exist to help people to be like this because they value and respect them. If these values are clear, then the kind of organization we develop for schools will facilitate their realization, not prevent this from happening.

In many ways the English primary school has been developing along lines that are sympathetic to OD values. The core consideration for the continuance of that development is how such schools deal with freedom — whether they help children to be free or whether they repress them. 1 do not mean this in a glib way for I know that freedom and responsibility go hand in hand. But the question is, if we do not allow freedom for all. Who is free to decide for others? OD is about the discovery of this freedom in its organizational manifestation. Once teachers accept the organizational implications, they still have to work on the personal and philosophical implications. Can it be that the consequence of liberal education is to frighten us and make us fearful of the freedom that we and others have begun to discover?

The Future

There is some evidence that OD will prove attractive to an increasingly large number of heads, particularly as they find traditional approaches to management wanting. Though most of the literature originates in the United States and is concerned with a somewhat different approach (a more highly structured technology) there is an increasing amount of writing about OD scattered throughout the various educational journals, some of it concerned with counselling approaches and innovative schemes in curriculum development. The journal *Educational Change and Development* is largely devoted to OD type approaches and the Network for Organization Development in Education (NODE) organizes an annual conference each Easter where educationists and others gather together to share ideas and experiences. In universities and polytechnics OD is familiar in programmes offered by departments of management,

While the term OD itself may not convey a full idea of what OD is about, many heads and senior teachers find that they have been working on OD values, and in an OD way when they talk together with OD 'professionals'. We can confidently predict that not only will OD change and develop itself but that many more people will come to understand what an OD view of organization means. In a period of considerable managerial crisis some of us believe that OD has the best answer yet. Certainly it is worth finding out more about it.

References

Gray, H.L. (1980) *Management in Education* Driffied, Nafferton; includes some accounts of OD interventions and underlying theory.

Miles, M.B. (1971) *Learning to Work in Groups* Teachers College Press; New York. One of the earliest handbooks for group work training, containing useful ideas for organizing training programmes and conducting meetings in school.

Schmuck, R., Runkel, P., Arends, J. and Arends, R. (1977) *The Second Handbook of Organization Development in Schools* Mayfield Publishing Co.; the classic American handbook. Well worth reading for a flavour of OD as it has developed. British readers may find some of the assumptions problematical.

There is also a journal *Educational Change and Development* that provides a running commentary on the scene with a strong UK bias. It is issued once a term. Further information from the Business Manager, Educational Change and Development, Department of Education Management, Sheffield City Polytechnic, 36 Collegiate Crescent, Sheffield, S10 3BP.

8
Progressive Education and Evaluation

> To be the best scientific observers we must at once be the best providers for and the best teachers of those whom we wish to study.
>
> (Hawkins 1974, p. 45)

But can a classroom teacher scientifically observe the learning processes of the students he teaches? There are those who would argue that even if he had the opportunity to do so, in terms of experience of theoretical issues and resources available, his observations would lack the objectivity which is claimed to be an essential feature of scientific inquiry. Others would suggest that it is only measurable behaviours — whether performance in objective tests or the frequency of certain categories of interaction — that can count as valid material from which inferences can be drawn about the learning process itself.

There is not the space here to enter into the arguments about the nature of scientific inquiry that are raised by such objections. But the experience of our programme of research and inservice training suggests that a combination of teaching and research roles can provide insight into the learning process from material which is largely inaccessible to the objective observer of classroom life. We find that teaching and research can in practice be complementary activities as Hawkins suggests. For not only does the researcher gain a greater degree of access to the ebb and flow of the students' learning through the close and sustained contact of teaching and learning with them, but the teacher is enabled to direct his input into the students' learning more sensitively by conducting the rigorous description and analysis that are essential features of research. Thus we might state the corollary of Hawkins' prescription: to be the best providers for and the best teachers we must at once be the best scientific observers of those whom we would teach.

We have attempted to combine the roles of teaching and research with pairs of teachers working together. One of the pair — the normal class teacher — tends to take on the major responsibility for managing the curriculum, while the visiting teacher/researcher is responsible for the research. But they share these tasks, the normal class teacher contributing to the gathering and analysis of material and the visiting teacher/researcher being fully involved in teaching alongside him. In practice, teaching and observation become largely indistinguishable activities. Daily fieldnotes which describe and analyze the students' work, together with samples of their writing, painting, models and so on, form the bulk of the research material.

First piloted in 1976, when Michael Armstrong came to work as teacher/researcher alongside the author in his primary school classroom, the programme now involves four teachers seconded to work alongside teachers in primary and secondary schools in the Leicestershire Classroom Research Inservice Training Scheme. (The first, pilot, phase is described in Armstrong, 1980, the second phase in Rowland, 1980). Also involved in the scheme are a further twenty-five teachers from a variety of schools who meet regularly to contribute material from their own classrooms and analyze it in groups. The work of this larger group not only provides a broader range of material from which developing theory may be corroborated, refuted or refined, but ensures that the issues upon which the research focuses, and the hypotheses which emerge, are both relevant and accessible to the classroom teacher. Since the teachers' contributions relate directly to their own classroom practice and serve to develop it, research and in-service training aspects become inseparable, with the teachers, in the final analysis, in control of both.

The broad aim of the research is to gain insight into the learning process and the quality of intellectual thought that is evidenced in the classroom. The descriptions, interpretations and evaluations which make up the research material take a form similar to that of the case study, with the work of individual students followed in detail. We do not aim to produce comprehensive generalizations, and our scope is very broad, but nevertheless a number of threads or issues have emerged to be of central significance. While these threads cannot yet be woven into a complete framework for understanding classroom learning, they do perhaps suggest the beginnings of such a framework.

There is not the space here to follow these threads in detail, but the research strategy and some of the implications for teaching may best be illustrated by reference to one of the issues that has emerged as being central to our findings. This concerns the nature of the relationship between teacher and student and the question of the student's autonomy within this relationship.

Researchers and educational commentators have often attempted to describe teaching styles in terms of the degree of autonomy which teachers permit and foster in their students. For example, the HMI report *Primary Education in England* (1978) conceived of the 'didactic' approach to teaching as one in which the organization of activities and the individual steps towards learning were clearly set out by the teacher, with the student following his lead. This approach was contrasted with the 'exploratory' approach in which 'the broad objectives of the work were discussed with the children but where they were then put in a position of finding their own solutions to the problems posed.' In practice, the report found, the individual teacher's overall style could be described in terms of a continuum between purely 'didactic' at one extreme and purely 'exploratory' at the other, with most teachers adopting an element of both approaches.

Our research suggests that this distinction (which may result from the observers' focus upon teachers and only the most readily accessible behaviour of their students) is unhelpful in describing the learning relationships between teacher and student. A more fundamental dimension to this relationship is not so much the degree to which the students are left to find their own solutions, but the extent to which they exert a control over their work, the nature of the teacher's collaboration in this, and the ways in which the student influences this collaboration. Our evidence suggests that where this controlling element on the part of the student is high, his activity is more likely to meet his intellectual needs and be appropriate to his level of experience (Rowland, 1979),

The nature of the control which the student may exercise might best be illustrated by examples of classroom activity as described and analyzed in research fieldnotes.

In this first example, Paula and Carol are working in an open plan primary school run on more or less informal lines. They are constructing a model camp site by building around frameworks of drinking straws jointed together with pipe-cleaners. Paula and Carol were both ten years old at the time and were two of a larger group of girls who would often work together.

Fieldnotes: 9 October (Monday)

On Firday Chris Harris (the normal class teacher) started off by talking to the class about work they might like to do connected to the theme 'School'. A poem was read and there was much discussion of the children's suggestions.

Carol and Paula wondered what it would be like if the school had not been built. What would the site of the school then have been used for? They suggested that it might be a campsite. Later they explained to me how there would be many tents where, on a fine night, children could come to sleep. Paula suggested that they would have to pay £1 a night to come and use the tents. She said there would also be a 'manager' who would live in the house alongside the camp site.

Carol and Paula had not been involved with some other children who had made various frameworks using drinking straws and pipe-cleaners the previous day. They had not seen the tent Jason had made using this technique, though they had seen one or two of the other structures. Paula's idea was that they could make tents by covering with tissue paper frameworks constructed out of drinking straws joined together with small pieces of pipe-cleaner.

By the time I came to watch them they had already made several tents. Some were based upon cubes, others upon long cuboids, others on square pyramids and there were various constructions of ridge rents (Figure 1).

Figure 1

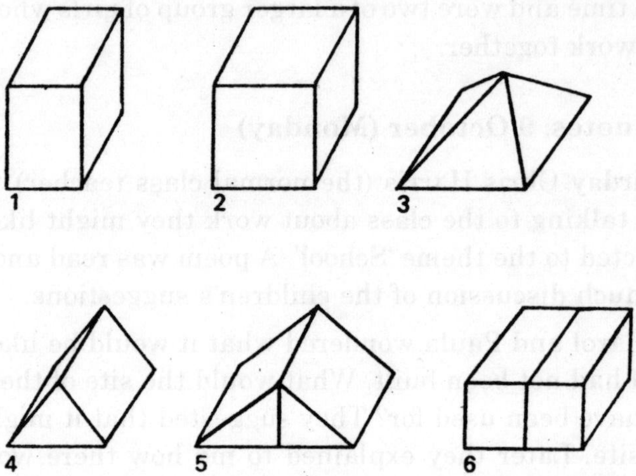

Each tent was covered with tissue paper, stuck down with glue, with entrances left open where required. They explained how tents like (1) were to be 'loos', the large tent like (2) was an 'entertainments tent' and the others were for sleeping. Another ridge tent they made but rejected saying that it was too large for their model. 'Look, it's even larger than the loos', Paula said. They felt that their ridage tents for sleeping in shou!d be smaller than the 'loo' tents.

Inside the 'loo' tents Carol had constructed little W.C. bowls. For these she had used two different constructions (Figure 2).

These frameworks were topped with tissue paper seats and accompanied by lavatory paper rolls made from pipe cleaners and tissue paper. Each tent bore the label 'Gents' or 'Ladies'.

Figure 2

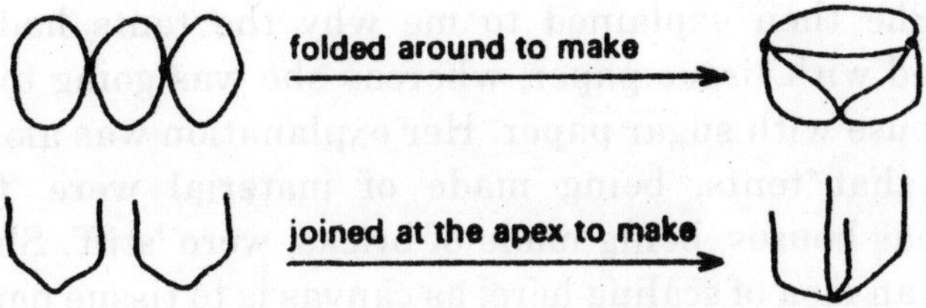

While Carol was experimenting with her seats, Paula was constructing 'The Manager's House'. This was to be a cuboid with a roof of trapezium cross section (Figure 3).

Figure 3

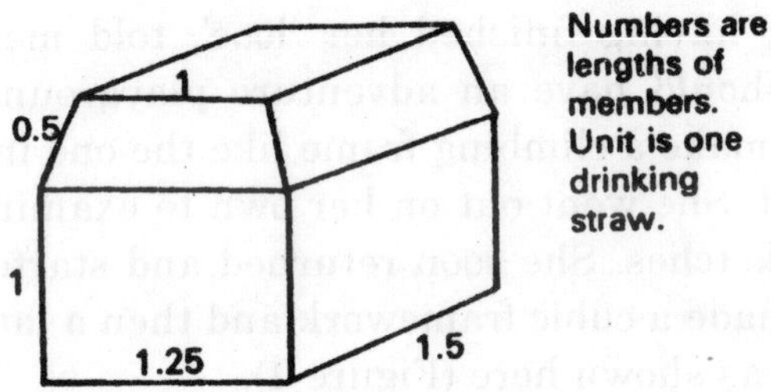

Paula worked confidently at this, measuring up each member against another of corresponding length, before jointing it into the structure. When she had finished the framework, she stood it up on the table. It stood firmly enough but was a bit lopsided. She examined it and explained how this would be put right by shortening one of the roof gable members. She quickly cut a bit off this straw and, after reassembling, the house stood upright. I was surprised how well this repair job had worked, but pointed out to her that while the house stood quite upright and firmly, now one of the roof members was shorter than its corresponding members. Paula replied that she didn't think we needed to be that fussy and that, while it wasn't quite right, it would do. I agreed.

She then explained to me why the tents had been covered with tissue paper, whereas she was going to cover the house with sugar paper. Her explanation was along the lines that tents, being made of material were 'flimsy' whereas houses, being made of bricks, were 'stiff'. She was using an idea of scaling here: as canvas is to tissue paper, so brick-work is to sugar paper. This notion of scaling pervades much of the children's model making, not only with regard to length. It cropped up in a different form when we came to test the various tents for how well they would stand up to strong winds. Paula blew on the tents, a strong puff representing a gale, a light blow a gentler breeze.

Carol, having finished her 'loos', told me how their campsite should have an adventure playground. For this she would make a climbing frame like the one in the school playground. She went out on her own to examine this, but made no sketches. She soon returned and started to build. First she made a cubic framework and then a lattice on one of its faces as shown here (Figure 4).

Figure 4

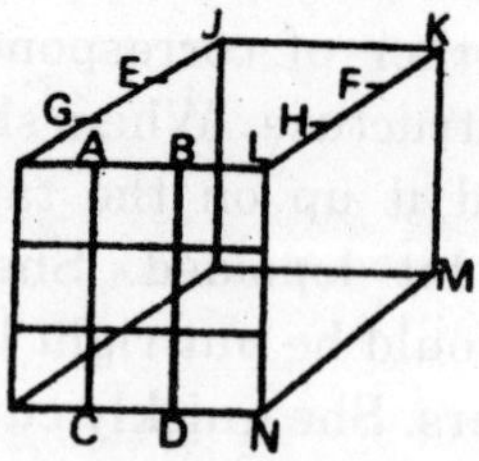

She explained to me: 'It's really a cube. You put two bits down like this (pointing to AC and BD) and then you cut out this bit (CD)'. She explained how this lattice on the front face was repeated in a vertical plane down from GH, EF and

JK. It was also the same, she said, on the face LKMN and its opposite face. (I later inspected the climbing frame in the playground more closely and, except for one small detail, her representation of it is quite correct). It seemed extraordinary that she was able to analyze the structure in such detail and keep the information in her mind. Could she have done this before she had started working on the tent frameworks? I should guess that her work so far had given her some insight, increased her conception and perception of the geometry of frameworks. What had perhaps, earlier, been seen as a mass of horizontal and vertical bars, was now seen as a cube together with its sub-divisions and missing elements. While one cannot be certain, this seems the most plausible explanation for her considerable insight and ability to remember the details of the structure. Just as, by representing our thoughts and feelings in words, we are more clearly to understand them, so by modelling, Carol increases her understanding of the spatial configurations which she represents. . . .

The following school day Paula and Carol continued to model the seats, lamp-posts, fountains, cash desk and till, telephone booth and other features of the campsite. The objects were then mounted on a piece of stiff cardboard (about 1m by 1.5m) and carefully arranged with pathways between the tents and so on.

The display is now very impressive. The light shines through the orange tissue paper of the restaurant tent onto the little tables (made of pipe-cleaners, plasticine and plastic lid) which are set out with minute silver paper knives and forks, candles and cardboard glasses. In the entertainments tent their favourite pop star (pipe-cleaners) performs into a microphone. Behind these tents were the 'Ladies' and 'Gents'. The climbing frame had been adapted so that it could have ropes hanging down from the central section. Near this is the telephone booth and, at the other end of the board, is the cluster of sleeping tents, paddling pool (a rectangle of silver card) and fountains. Lamp-posts stand amongst the tents.

Paula said that their model was 'Paradise'. But after discussing it amongst themselves they decided not to call it Paradise Camp Site. Laraine (who had now joined to help them) had said, 'It's going to be Luxury here' and they finally decided to call it 'Mount Posh'. Thus the little sign in front of the model which says, 'Welcome to Mount Posh'. . . .

Now that all the individual items are assembled it looks not only charming but surprisingly realistic. Their attention to scale has been precise throughout. They have also used considerable ingenuity in overcoming difficulties as they arose. For example, the restaurant tables could not be supported by the thin straws alone, so each straw had been re-inforced by inserting a pipe-cleaner down its length. . . .

The level of teacher intervention throughout this work was minimal. The two original ideas — the technique of jointing drinking straws with pipe-cleaners and the School theme — had both been provided by teachers but in different contexts and on different days. Neither I nor Chris Harris had envisaged that they would be combined in this or any other way. Carol and Paula chose to respond to these two separate ideas by using them to construct what turned out to be their own fantasy world. Within such a world and the process of its construction I, as a teacher, played no significant part. While the girls were only too happy to talk to me about what they had done, my assistance (except in a few matters of material provisioning) was not required. This was not because the task they had set themselves was easy — on the contrary, it presented many considerable challenges — but because within their 'Paradise' they were the final arbiters upon whose judgments the value of the work depended. I was at best merely a sympathetic and interested outsider. This independence from my judgments was clearly demonstrated by Paula insisting that my criticism of her house was inappropriate: 'we needn't be that fussy'. From the delicacy and ingenuity of her constructions and her concern for such aspects as scale, it is clear that such a rejection of my tentative criticism was not merely a reflection of a lack of precision in her working style.

Their work was thus their own in the broadest sense. Their control over its purposes and methods was ultimate. When, at one point, we discussed the names of the various shapes they had made (cube, cuboid, prism, trapezium, etc.) they were fascinated to learn them as applied to their shapes, shapes which had now become part of their everyday and imaginary experience. During the process of their work they needed to conceive of geometrical abstractions. There is little doubt that their ability to do this developed in response to the needs of the present task. No one had designed the task in order to develop these specific skills. When [had introduced the technique of making jointed frameworks to some other children the previous day, I did have in mind that spatial ideas might emerge. But no one had suggested that Carol or Paula should use this technique and they had not been present when 1 demonstrated it.

Was this development just a matter of good luck ? Clearly some play-like activities are more productive of significant learning than others. The work of Paula and Carol is not presented here as part of a claim that all play is educationally significant, or even that play should form a major part of the activity of a class of nine to eleven years old but simply that some play, of which this was an example, clearly enables considerable learning to take place within a situation in which the children have complete control over their activity and in which the involvement of any adult is minimal. There may have been many types of learning associated with this particular activity, stemming from the social context and its imaginative and representational aspects, but attention is here drawn to the development of spatial awareness : how they learned the names of several geometric shapes, investigated certain of their properties and increased their understanding of three dimensional space.

The structure of this learning activity may be represented thus:

Schema 1

Children select stimuli to which they respond	→	Children set task	→	They develop specific concepts/skills required by the task

Such a schema may be contrasted with that which describes practical activities which are structured by the teacher. For then the teacher decides upon certain specific concepts or skills which he feels require development ; a practical task is set such that the children encounter or practice these skills or concepts; the child performs the task and thus acquires the required learning. This may be represented :

Schema 2

T. decides skills/sets concepts	→	T. designs/ sets appropriate task	→	Ch. performs task	→	Ch. acquires specified learning

Schema 1 may be characterized as 'natural' learning, or learning which results from the children following 'the impulses inherent in childhood itself (Piaget, 1969, p, 151). The links between the stages take place naturally and there is no question of the appropriateness of the skills/concepts to their activity. Nor is there any question of interpretation of the task or of its interest value. Once the sequence has begun it is limited only by the extent of the children's present experience and knowledge, but it serves to extend both.

On the other hand, an activity which follows scheme 2 may be limited by :

(a) The appropriateness of the decision to teach these specific concepts/skills to the stage of development, experience and interests of the child.

(b) The appropriateness of these concepts/skills in terms of the curriculum.

(c) The design of the task set : its suitability for furthering these particular skills/concepts.

(d) The possibility that the child will not interpret and internalize the nature of the task as the teacher intended.

This second schema is the basis for most curriculum design and much activity planning. Its success depends upon a high level of diagnosis of the individual children, knowledge of the subject-matter and its relationship to the curriculum and to child development, ability to design or select appropriate tasks and to communicate them unambiguously. Attempts have been made to overcome these difficulties, or rather to bypass them, by programmed learning. But such techniques are appropriate only to skills and concepts which can be precisely defined and even then they tend not to stimulate their application to activities outside the structured course itself (that is, there is the problem of transference).

Schema 1 also has its problems. Learning cannot be left merely to the chance responses of the students to the environment. Even if children frequently do learn in this way there remains the problem not only of providing a stimulating environment but also of ensuring that they develop a comprehensive range of skills and knowledge. This requires the teacher to be more than merely a provisioner of the learning environment.

It is not suggested that classroom learning should follow the first 'play' schema rather than the second 'teacher-structured' one, but that, in his relationship with the child and his work, the teacher may exploit the child's natural tendency to learn, a tendency which is demonstrated in much of their play.

An essential feature of the 'play' schema, which is usually lacking in the 'teacher-structured' approach, is the degree of control which the student is able to exert over his activity. By 'control' is meant not only autonomy in the choice of the activity but also in respect of interpretations made in its course, its further development and overall objectives. Our observations suggest that where the student exercises control, his activities develop rationally in response to events as they arise while he bears in mind certain overall objectives. Thus the student's exercise of control involves a structuring to his activity. In the work of Carol and Paula, this structuring took place without significant intervention on the part of the teacher.

But clearly the teacher's contribution is often going to be more positive than in the example above. In his attempts to introduce the student to new areas of study, to provide opportunity for the development of particular skills or perhaps in order to stimulate enthusiasm, the teacher may take a more deliberate lead. In such cases, our evidence suggests that what is important is not so much whether the teacher adopts a 'didactic' approach (leading the student step by step through a process) or an 'exploratory' one (leaving him to find his own solutions having discussed the broad objectives) but rather the way in which he hands over a degree of control to the student. Once established, this control is not of an exclusive nature, indeed it may demand not only the teacher's collaboration but even his formal instruction (Rowland, 1981). Furthermore, through such exercise of control on the student's part, the teacher is able to gain insight into the nature of his understanding, increased awareness of the ways in which he interprets his learning environment and, thereby, to contribute to this environment in a more fruitful way.

But where the teacher takes this initiative in the student's activity, the handing over of control to him may present problems, A teacher who is over anxious to ensure that all areas of the curriculum are covered, that certain 'standards' are achieved, may feel that he cannot afford to do this; that it would leave too much to chance. The problem remains whether the teacher's enthusiasm results from such external pressures or from his own more personal values or interests. On many occasions have I entered the classroom with 'exciting ideas' to 'get the children going' and they soon take on my enthusiasm in the new work. But then, as the work proceeds, it becomes increasingly clear that the children have built up a dependency upon me. While they are keen to follow and act upon my ideas, they seem unable to conjure up any of their own. I become firmly established at the centre of the stage and cannot withdraw to the wings without the show collapsing. At the end of the experience we may all feel that it has been enjoyable but it has somehow got us nowhere. The question remains: 'and what next?'

From this we should not conclude that the teacher should restrain his enthusiasm. Indeed, it should be infectious and inspire the kind of independent learning desired. The problem arises because of a failing in the relationship between the teacher, the learner and the subject-matter. 'Adults and children, like adults with each other, can associate well only in worthy interests and pursuits, only through a community of subject-matter which extends beyond the circle of their intimacy' (Hawkins, 1974, p. 49). As long as the subject-matter is not seen as the possession of the teacher, as long as he is not seen by the students (or himself) as having sole access to it, then he will be able to be sensitive to the student's interpretations and reactions, to value these and to help the student to develop the activity according to them. Only then will the learner be able to regain control of the process of his own learning, while the teacher becomes, as Bruner puts it, 'part of the student's internal dialogue' (Bruner, 1966, p. 124). Later in the same book, he says, 'To isolate the major difficulty, then, I would say that while a body of knowledge is given life and direction by the conjectures and dilemmas that brought it into being and sustained its growth, pupils who are being taught often do not have a corresponding sense of conjecture and dilemma' (*ibid.*, p. 159). It is the opportunity for such conjecture and dilemma that is the key to the student's retaining or gaining control over his activity. Our observations suggest that, when this opportunity is offered, children are indeed able to make the most of it and strive to do so, in order to control their work. As soon as a child says, I wonder what would happen if....?' or 'How could this be so?' he has begun to define his problems, the essence of his control over the work.

This point concerning the problem of the teacher's handing over control to the student may be illustrated by a sequence of activity which involved David and Greg. I had been stimulated by some conversations with a mathematician, and my own reading, on aspects of the famous Fibonacci series. (This is a series of numbers which has many strange properties, some of which are not yet altogether understood.) From the outset of my introducing some of these ideas to David and Greg, I was only too aware that, while there seemed to be unlimited potential here for children to explore, it would not be easy for me to hand over control to them. Certain techniques and approaches to constructing and analyzing the series needed to be followed if anything fruitful was to emerge. The problem seemed to be one of introducing such techniques in a way which did not then cast me in the role of the one who 'knows all the answers' and therefore force a dependence of the children upon me. In my enthusiasm for the investigations I also had to make a conscious effort to be receptive to what they thought about what we were doing and not to get carried away on my own path.

Fieldnotes: (12 October)

... I started working with David and Greg, two friends who are interested in numbers though they have no particularly striking skills in formal aspects of arithmetic.

I first explained the rule for forming a Fibonacci series. Starting with the terms 1, 1, each terms is made by adding together the two previous terms:

1, 1, 2, 3, 5, 8, 13, 21, 34, 55, 89, ...

We made this series together and spent some time examining it, seeing how its terms grew. It soon became apparent to me that the arithmetic involved could be made much simpler by reducing each term to a single digit by adding the digits in its number (thus 13 becomes 4 and the 8th term would then be $8 + 4 \rightarrow 12 \rightarrow 3$). With Greg acting as scribe and David checking the calculations, they transformed the above Fibonacci Series into a Reduced Fibonacci Series :

1, 1, 2, 3, 5, 8, 4, 3, 7, 1, 8, 9, 8, 8, 7, 6, 4, 1, 5, 6, 2, 8, 1, 9, 1, 1, 2, 3.

When they got this far they realized that the last four terms were the same as the first four and that the series was repeating itself.

David and Greg clearly needed some help with analyzing this series. 1 suggested that we count the number of terms in the first cycle of the series, cut the series into two halves (12 terms in each half) and add together corresponding terms in each half. Like this :

1 1 2 3 5 8 4 3 7 1 8 9   8 8 7 6 4 1 5 6 2 8 1 9

First term in first half + First term in second half =1+ 8 9

Second term in first half + Second term in second half =1+ 8 9

Third term in first half + Third term in second half =2+ 7 9 and so on, with the sum of each pair being 9.

None of us could explain why this 9 repeated itself, but David and Greg were obviously excited by the discovery. It seemed to me better at this stage to help them to find more such patterns before attempting to untangle the reasons for them.

Greg then suggested that we make another series the same way but starting with 2, 2 instead of 1, 1. He did this, with David watching and checking his figures. Again, he found that the series repeated itself after 24 terms.

The rest of yesterday afternoon was spent constructing similar series starting with (3, 3); (4, 4) and so on up to (9, 9). I suggested recording these series in the form of a matrix. Greg worked at this slowly and accurately. David left all the calculating to Greg, preferring to concentrate on picking out the various patterns which emerged.

At the end of the day they both decided to take home large sheets of squared paper on which to continue the work. Greg was going to write up the results so far. David would try to make up a new series.

The next morning (this morning) David told me how he had 'got stuck.' In fact a small arithmetical error had thrown his series out. Greg had completed the matrix like this:

and so on

```
        [1 1] 2 3 5 8 4 3 7 1 8 9 [8 8] 7 6 4 1 5 6 2 8 1 9 [1 1] →
        [2 2] 4 6 1 7 8 6 5 2 7 9 [7 7] 5 3 8 2 1 3 4 7 2 9 [2 2] →
        [3 3] 6 9 6 6 3 9 3 3 6 9 [6 6] 3 9 3 3 6 9 6 6 3 9 [3 3] →
        [4 4] 8 3 2 5 7 3 1 4 5 9 [5 5] 1 6 7 4 2 6 8 5 4 9 [4 4] →
        [5 5] 1 6 7 4 2 6 8 5 4 9 [4 4] 8 3 2 5 7 3 1 4 5 9 [5 5] →
        [6 6] 3 9 3 3 6 9 6 6 3 9 [3 3] 6 9 6 6 3 9 3 3 6 9 [6 6] →
        [7 7] 5 3 8 2 1 3 4 7 2 9 [2 2] 4 6 1 7 8 6 5 2 7 9 [7 7] →
        [8 8] 7 6 4 1 5 6 2 8 1 9 [1 1] 2 3 5 8 4 3 7 1 8 9 [8 8] →
        [9 9] 9 9 9 9 9 9 9 9 9 9 [9 9] 9 9 9 9 9 9 9 9 9 9 [9 9] →
[10 10] [1 1] 2 3 5 8 4 3 7 1 8 9 [8 8] 7 6 4 1 5 6 2 8 1 9 [1 1] →
```

and underneath had written:

"The top and bottom row of our pattern both have exactly the same numbers because: [l0 10 | 2 tens are wrong but [l l] 'two' 'ones' are right because we are only using Single Figured numbers. You may be amazed to see a whole line of nines this is because 9 + 9 = 18 well 1+8 = 9 you see 18 is 10 + 8, and 10 + 8 = 18".

We had only talked briefly yesterday about the final 10, 10, → 1, 1, series. Note here that while Greg's style of writing is precise and logical, it is highly personal: 'You may be amazed to see ... well .. . you see.' Though such comments are not part of the nature of a mathematical proof, here they appropriately demonstrate Greg's excitement and close identification with the ideas he expresses.

The 'boxed' numbers represent the pattern which David spotted yesterday. He also pointed out the column of third terms (that is, 2, 4, 6, 8, 1, 3, .. .) explaining that this was really 'going up in twos, the 1 and 3 really meaning 10 and 12.' (They did not realize at this point that indeed every column is a 'times table.' reduced.) By now David, who had not done much in the way of calculating yesterday, decided to leave us so that he could work out for himself all the series we had made so far. I was surprised at his decision. I had expected him to avoid the hard work and only to get involved in the pattern spotting. But now he apparently realized that the activity had many possibilities and he would rather practise the appropriate technical skills before progressing further. So he went off without any of Greg's figures to do it all over again for himself. Only once or twice did he ask for my help after suspecting he had made a mistake because the patterns he had in mind were not coming out right.

So far Greg had been very much led by me in this work. He fully understood everything and worked out the calculations himself, but had not had any ideas of his own for further exploration. Hoping to encourage him to branch out more, I suggested that, if he wanted to make more series, he could either change the rule of construction (that is, replace the 'add two previous terms' rule of the Fibonacci Series by some other rule) or change the initial terms. He decided on the latter and, using the same rule, started another Reduced Fibonacci Series with (1, 2). He soon saw that his new series was merely the (1, 1) series displaced by one term (that is, 1, 2, 3, 5 ... instead of 1, 1, 2, 3). Pleased by this, he started again with (2, 3). Again he soon saw that this was the original (1, 1) series, but this time displaced by two terms (that is, 2, 3, 5, 8 ... instead of 1, 1, 2, 3, ...). His next series he started with (3, 4). This he completed until it began to repeat after 24 terms. Then the same starting with (4, 5) until this also repeated after 24 terms.

We then looked closely at our original matrix of series. I pointed out that the numbers (3, 4) appear adjacent to one another in the matrix as the 8th and 9th terms of the series beginning (7, 7). Greg noticed that his new (3, 4) series was merely a continuation from that point in the (7, 7) series. Similarly, we found that his new (4, 5) series was a continuation from the 10th and llth terms of the (4, 4) series in our matrix.

We then saw that our original matrix contained every possible combination of two digits adjacent to one another and thus that any Reduced Fibonacci Series starting with any two digits could be found within that matrix.

By now we were treading on ground quite new to both of us. l had not envisaged all this. Greg was enthralled. He said, 'It contains everything. It must be magic!'

Greg then said he would change the construction rule. 'I am now going to add on certain numbers. I don't think you'll understand that'. (Even in this chat, he is concerned that his meaning may not be quite clear). He then showed me what he meant. It would be a straightforward arithmetical progression starting with 2 and adding 2 for each term, reducing to single digits in the usual way. Thus:

2, 4, 6, 8, 1, 3 ...

And saw, with amazement, that this also occurred in the original matrix as the 3rd column. (He had forgotten that David had pointed out this feature yesterday).

He then made a similar progression in threes (3, 6, 9, 3 . ...) and saw that this corresponded to the 4th column of the matrix. He then saw that any such arithmetical séries (or 'table') was represented in the columns of the matrix.

Then Greg said, 'I'm going to think of something that might not be here,' (in the matrix). After some thought, he explained how he would make a series by adding the two previous terms and then adding 5 to this result. Thus after the two initial terms (5, 5) the third would not be 1 (5 + 5 → 10 → 1) but 6 (1 × 5 → 6). Each term would be similarly increased by 5 after adding the two previous terms. He soon had written:

5, 5, 6, 7, 9, 3, 8, 7, 2, 5, 3, 4, 3, 3, 2, 1, 8, 5, 9, I, 6 ...

and said, 'Come on. I want to see 5, 5 again'. Sure enough, the series repeated as he had expected after 24 terms:

... 3, 5, 4, (5, 5)

and, as Greg had intended, this series did not occur in his matrix.

Greg employed various strategies to further analyze this series, breaking it into halves, then quarters, adding corresponding terms and so on. This produced no further clear patterns. (Although had Greg used exactly the same strategy as I had used in analyzing our first Reduced Fibonacci Series he would have found a repeating number). But after various manipulations with the figures he ended up with four terms 8, 2, 4, 1. I pointed out to him the doubling relationship between these terms and Greg said, 'Yes, double it! That's given me an idea' and proceeded to explain how a new rule for construction could be: double previous term and reduce to single figure (that is, a geometric progression).

He went off to work on his own and soon returned to show me what he had done.

3 6 3 6 3 6

1 2 4 8 7 5 (1 2 4 8 7 5)

2 4 8 7 5 1 (2 4 8 7 5)

4 8 7 5 1 2 (4 8 7 5)

5 1 2 4 8 7 (5 1) (Note 5 and 1)

6 3 (6 3 6) (Note 6 and 3)

7 5 1 2 4 8 (7 5)

His words 'Note' refer to the displaced identity between series starting with 5 and 1 and between those starting with 3 and 6. The brackets suggest the repeating nature of the series. When we examined these series together we saw that every series except those starting with either (3), (6) or (9) is identical except displaced. Greg pointed out that the doubling series starting with (9) would simply be 9, 9, 9 ... (that is. 9, 18, 36, 72 ... → 9, 9, 9, 9 . . ,). He then said the series starting with 10 would really be a series starting with 1.

He then said, 'If we were enormously clever we could triple them', that is, produce tripling geometric series.

He worked on his own while I watched. He completed this :

1	3	9	9	9	...	He saw that since 9 × 3 = 27 → 9 and
2	6	9	9		...	27 × 3 = 81 → 9, once 9 occurred in the
3	9A	9			...	series, it would simply continue to repeat
4	3B	9			...	itself.
5	6	9			...	When he had got as far as (A) he said,
6	9	9			...	referring to the second column of the
7	3	9			...	emerging matrix, 'Look, it's 3, 6, 9 again'.
8	6	9			...	And at (B) 'We're just going to start
9	9	9			...	again' (that is, the column will repeat itself).

Meanwhile David, working on his own, had completed the matrix of Reduced Fibonacci Series. It was near the end of the afternoon and he said, 'When I go home I'm going to make a new one'. He said he would start with (9, 9) and use the rule of adding the two previous terms and also 2 to this sum (that is, similar to Greg's invented series which David had watched him make). He said, 'This is going to be easy. It'll just be ; 9 9 2 2 2 ...' I asked him why. He said that since 9 + 9 → 18 and 18 + 2 → 20 → 2 the next term would be 2 which would just repeat itself. Suspecting his reasoning here, I suggested he do it now. He was keen to, and soon saw that his hypothesis was wrong as the series started : 9, 9, 2, 4, 8 ... He said, 'You've gotta make mistakes. It'll go back to 9, 9 anyway. I'll make it!' In spite of his mistake, he does not lack confidence and feels quite in control of the situation.

Sure enough, after 24 terms, David's series did start to repeat itself.

And so ended two days of arithmetic. David and Greg said they had enjoyed it very much. David had earlier shown some concern as to whether this would help them when they get to their secondary school next year. I said I thought it would. Thereupon they decided to spend three days a week doing 'this kind of maths'. 'We'd need a break sometimes', added Greg.

They did indeed go on to do much more work on this (though their decision to work on it three days a week was a little extravagant!). They went on to develop more series and explored ways of transforming them into straight line patterns.

No doubt much was gained by all three of us from this work. It certainly affected David and Greg's approach to arithmetic, now they saw numbers as 'beings' which had a certain mystique. This seems to be the underlying emotional response of the pure mathematician. The fact that the numbers did not count things did not mean that they were the meaningless abstractions which is often the case with 'sums'.

But throughout the first day of work, I was very much the performer and leader of the discoveries. While they did make their own series and spot patterns emerging, each development of the activity was initiated by myself. They were completely dependant upon me. This was demonstrated by the fact that the work Greg did at home after the first day was simply a repeat of what had been done with me. I do not mean to imply that it was therefore of no value, but that it demonstrates his inability, or disinclination, in spite of considerable enthusiasm, to take the work further on his own.

On the second day, David's decision to go off on his own and practise the technique of building series is a clear indication of his desire to make the work his own, to control it and to reduce his dependency upon me (and Greg) in making the necessary calculations.

The point at which Greg really began to exercise his control in the work is clearly seen. In the middle of the second day, after we had made Reduced Fibonacci Series starting with every possible combination of two figures, I noted, 'By now we were treading on ground quite new to *both* of us'. And then, only two lines later: 'Greg then said he would change the construction rule'. From this point onwards the nature of the series investigated branched out considerably, no longer following the Fibonacci rule of construction. Greg proceeded to initiate a sequence of investigations, inventions and hypotheses based upon a now heightened awareness of what a series is and some good approaches to discovering its pattern-making potential.

Is it really a coincidence that Greg started to take the initiative in his enquiries at the very point at which I also felt that I was treading on new ground? It seems that the freshness of the discoveries for me cast me in a truly collaborative role, rather than in a primarily leading one in which I possessed all the clues to the progress of the work. From this point the investigations took on a sense of spontaneity similar to that of an art as characterized by Dewey : 'The spontaneous in art is complete absorption in subject-matter that is fresh, the freshness of which holds and sustains the emotion' (Dewey, 1934, p. 70).

Of course it would be unrealistic to suppose that each time we initiate an activity, or offer specific instruction or guidance, we can expect the student to make discoveries which are in every sense new to us. Usually we shall have trodden the ground before the student reaches it. But there is a strong sense in which as soon as he begins to tackle real problems, problems as he has constructed or interpreted them, then the learning that takes place and the knowledge which is gained is not merely a copy of the teacher's knowledge, but is a reconstruction of it. Such knowledge may view the same objective world and concern itself with the same facts, but will offer a perspective upon them which is individual and to that extent unique and new.

The two illustrations I have used relate to activities of a more or less mathematical nature. These were chosen because it appears that it is within the mathematics curriculum that children are most frequently denied the opportunity to exercise a controlling influence over their work. Many observations of children's writing, art and scientific investigations appear to confirm that learning is an active process of construction or reconstruction in which the student's control is of fundamental importance.

While this direction in our findings might be seen as reinforcing a 'progressive' rather than a 'traditional' approach to teaching, its implications go far beyond the questions of classroom organization and 'teaching style' that are normally seen as defining a 'progressive' approach. It suggests an epistemology which rejects the view that knowledge is absolute and objective, a commodity which can be possessed by the teacher and replicated in the student. On the other hand knowledge must have its roots in society: it is more than merely the description of the psychological state of the knower.

Such issues may seem to be highly philosophical considerations of little concern to the classroom teacher. But the analysis of students' work by an expanding group of teachers is leading us to consider such matters more seriously as a basis and rationale for our developing classroom practice.

The final objective of any educational research is to enable change to take place as a result of an increase in our understanding. An advantage of the research method reported here is that this change takes place in the process of the research. It is through his researching that the teacher is enabled to improve his teaching. The means and the ends of the research thus largely coincide.

References

Armstrong, M. (1981) *Closely Observed Children,* London, Writers and Readers Publishing Corp.

Bruner, J.S. (1966) *Toward a Theory of Instruction* Cambridge, Mass., Harvard University Press.

Her Majesty's Inspectorate (1978) *Primary Education in England: A Survey by HM Inspectors of Schools* London, HMSO.

Dewey, J. (1934) *Art as Experience* New York, Minton Balch.

Hawkins, D. (1974) *The Informed Vision:.Essays on Learning and Human Nature* New York, Agathon.

Piaget, J. (1969) *Science of Education and the Psychology of Child* Longman, London, p. 151.

Rowland, S.C.W. (1979) 'Ability matching: A critique' *Forum for the Discussion of New Trends in Education* 21(3), pp. 82- 86.

Rowland, S.C.W. (1980) 'Enquiry into classroom learning' unpublished MED thesis, Leicester University.

Rowland, S C. W. (1981) 'How to intervene: Clues from the work of a 10 year old' *Forum for the Discussion of New Trends in Education* 23(2), pp. 3-8.

9
The Evaluation of Citizenship

Possibly one of the most difficult problems the typical teacher faces is the evaluation of the complex curriculum known and the social studies. Involved in the evaluation of this subject are not only objective criteria such as grades and arithmetic levels of achievement, but also the large element of subjectivity. The subjective characters of the evaluation may very well take a wide variety of forms. The introduction of subjective evaluations has unfortunately been neglected by most writers in this particular field.

Cummings states that :

The growth of evaluation has been one of the major achievements in American education during the last two decades. Evaluation of citizenship education has been a part of that movement. In general, broad objectives have been agreed upon, and evaluation has been an attempt to discover to what extent these objectives are being reached.

However, research in evaluation discloses that Cumming's statement is subject to some question. Other writers such as Otto contend.

Unfortunately most current efforts at evaluation of instruction in the social studies are restricted to methods of appraising what children have learned in social studies without also examining and appraising the transfer of these learnings, or of some of them, to the events of everyday living.

Undoubtedly Otto has more particularly appreciated the difficulties involved in the evaluation of the social studies than been indicated in the rather broad generalization of Cummings.

The social studies encompass a diverse categorization of individual subjects which can be interrelated into a meaningful whole. The subjects included in the social studies have come to mean, "those portions of history, geography, civics, and other social sciences that are selected for use in teaching. "In addition the term in many areas also includes, '. . . the social sciences, art, literature, music, and even some phases of science." The ultimate goal of the social studies is directed toward generating and improving individual student citizenship.

Progress in the social studies should be evaluated in terms of the teaching objectives. Instruction in the social studies for the purpose of developing:

"Responsible, sensitive, and courageous citizens who will participate intelligently in the solving of problems growing out of their own human relationships and problems facing society.

Accurate knowledge of man and society. Informed insight into man and society. Those skills essential to acquiring knowledge and insight.

Loyalty to social ideals that forward the dignity of individual men and the brotherhood of all men.

Ability to apply knowledge, insight, skill and loyalty to daily living.

Familiarity with urgent social problems such as the dangerous spread between mechanical and social invention, provincial nationalism that blocks progress toward "one world", the confusion between education and propaganda and wastefulness in the use of natural resources.

Personality traits in the child through meeting his needs for exploration, muscle activity, social activity, imaginative activity, and recognition as an individual."

It is evident that evaluation of progress toward such goals will require a broader base than recitations and tests.The development of an evaluation technique of the social studies subjects is the major objective of this paper. Evaluation consists of the determination of the level of achievement, appreciation, understanding, and accomplishment on the part of the student. As previously indicated a series of objective criteria is satisfactory but by no means completely indicative as an attainment measure.

"Evaluation includes measurement but it extends far beyond the areas to which objective measurements have been applied".

An attempt to develop subjective criteria for evaluation is presented which will prove more revealing and significant to the teacher for purposes of more fully ascertaining the true level of achievement on the part of the student.

A brief presentation of some past and unfortunately existing evaluation procedures may well be in order so that a highlighting of current defects can be indicated. Generally speaking a separatist treatment of each of the individual subjects in the broad social studies field has prevailed. Recent advances indicate that a fusionism of these many subjects into a coordinated whole develops a better and more integrated appreciation on the part of the student.

Antediluvian conceptualizations which are largely disappearing from the scene stressed regimentation, rote learning, and memorization of factual data to an extreme degree. Obvious defects in such methodology have been recognized and attempts to correct them have been introduced through the idea of integration or fusionistic philosophies. Obvious defects developed from these conceptualizations which were primarily manifest in the form of lack of student interest, inability to evaluate the over-all impact of the several subjects, questionable value to the student, and in all probability, a complete lack of recall on the part of the student after the passage of a very short period of time.

Presently the trend toward integration of the social studies presents an attempt to counteract the disadvantages inherent in classical doctrines. Most advanced present thought appears to be centered on the philosophy of making the social studies significant, meaningful, and developing better and more informed citizens. These latter developments are definitely worthy of praise as being forward steps in attaining the before-mentioned objectives. However, current with the new philosophy is introduced the problem to which this paper is devoted, namely, that of evaluation. It is admitted that evaluation under classical dogma practices was a much simpler and more objective procedure.

However, evaluation of the social studies under our new integrated and fusionistic teaching methodology does present some extremely complex and, as previously indicated, undeveloped evaluation problems.

Questions such as: How do we weigh the increase or decrease in individual student citizenship? How do we evaluate the impact of integrated social studies on making the student a more understanding and better member of society? What percentage should we assign to a student's grade for the positive factor which could be generated out of a well developed social studies program, namely a reduction in racial discrimination? When do we know, and what percentage should be given to a student's grade to indicate his achievement of attitudes which are socially harmonious? What grade is assignable to evidences of maturity and ability on the part of the student to appreciate contemporary social structures?

Questions such as these introduce the before-mentioned subjective evaluation factors. No objective type of examination can ever possibly reveal a representative answer to any of the foregoing questions. It can be appreciated that the classical methodology previously indicated is helpless in generating a meaningful answer to any of these questions. From a review of the brief foregoing discussions it appears that the elimination of subjective factors from the grading of social studies achievement is quite impossible. A concentration or a misdirection of emphasis on objective factors will only develop non-representation and probably misleading results.

Evaluation is therefore divisible into subjective and objective grading elements. The objective elements have been classified by several authorities in this field.

Otto mentions that, "In some schools teachers have become so 'measurement conscious' that they have discarded the use of teacher observation as a means of identifying children's, problems and noting children's development. In such schools little attention is paid to any information or evidence which cannot be classified, tabulated, and treated statistically. Measurement has an important place in educational work, but so does teacher observation of pupil behaviour and performance."

The Association of Social Studies Teachers of the City of New York reveals that,

Any analysis of examinations currently in use in the social studies would reveal an emphasis on the testing of the mastery of information. Since there is universal acceptance of the wider objectives in teaching to include not only information but also skills and attitudes, an undisputed answer to the query, "What to Test?" Should be that examinations must test all the objectives of teaching, information, skills and attitudes.

The following factors should be considered in order to develop skills and attitudes:

"1. Reading and interpretation of graphs.
2. Map making and reading.
3. Use of reference materials.
4. Participation in panel discussions, debates, etc.
5. Writing dramatizations, diaries, etc.
6. Observations as a result of trips.
7. Making of posters, cartoons, graphs, etc. to illustrate some phase of the subject-matter.
8. Preparing materials for visual exhibit.
9. Preparing outlines and presenting reports.
10. Ability to analyze material being presented with one's own knowledge.
11. Ability to listen to a speaker and determine what to listen for.
12. Ability to make and take notes for later reference and study."

The most outstanding limitation of standardized as well as teacher-made tests is the lack of attention given to the measurement of understanding of concepts and generalizations.

. . . .observation of behaviour and evaluation in any area becomes difficult without some normative frame of reference and some reasonably objective or tangible criteria.

Evaluation of the social program should be carried on as continuously and persistently as evaluation of the child's learning. In fact, the appraisal of outcomes of learning experiences in the social studies inevitably leads to evaluation of the program. Such evaluation, however, is sometimes neglected because comprehensive criteria are not used.

Factual tests are easier to make, easier to score, and, in a sense, easier to defend than any other type of test.

Subjective ascertainment levels are not as easily indentifiable as indicated in the quotes from the above authorities. The subjective evaluation is founded on the interpretative and analytical talents of the grader. Answers to the previously developed questions can only be developed in the light of three basic criteria.

First the student has to demonstrate that he comprehends the basic factual material in the social studies group. Indication of this comprehension ability is developed through the criteria of tests and examinations. This first components of the overall evaluation process is objective in nature.

Subjectivity is introduced in the second and third components in the form of personal judgment. The second and third components of.the subjective evaluation process are namely, the applications of the learned material and finally a measures of consistency in the application itself.

Individual observation will demonstrate whether or not the student is applying the principles for which he has demonstrated comprehension. The application is demonstrable in a variety of forms. For instance, a student may well be able to correctly answer an examination question such as : Is racial segregation basically undemocratic ? Comprehension is demonstrated here. However, the examination answer is not entirely indicative of the final degree of citizenship possessed by the student. Observation of the student in his social environment and contact with others will reveal whether or not a satisfactory degree of comprehension exists.

The point being developed here is that the individual observation of the teacher directed toward uncovering evidences of application or non-application is necessary before the ascertainment of a grade can be realistically developed.

The third component of our subjective criteria, namely consistency, is more or less self explanatory. The comprehension of factual data and its subsequent degree of application has to be consistently applied before a proper evaluation can be determined. A student correctly saying that racial segregation is undemocratic and applying the principle in his social activities must demonstrate a level and degree of consistency before a grader could rank him in the highest stratum of a particular group.

Thus it can be seen that a subjective evaluation incorporates not only objective but also subjective measures which require individual observation. The ultimate goal is to develop better citizens through the consistent application of basic teachings associated in the social studies group.

A selection of three cases with which the writer has had experience is presented in order to further clarify the subjective evaluation technique.

Case A

John, a boy of 12 years of age, demonstrated exceptionally high ability in every examination. His grades in all subjects were A's. He was never absent or late, personable, and at all times a neatly dressed individual. Unfortunately, John was unable to play with other children. He was quite egotistical and the offspring of an extremely wealthy family. Observation revealed that he was extremely class and race conscious, and although a brilliant student, quite unable to get along with any of the other students in the school. He refused to enter into any group activities, would not talk to or associate with any of the other students. He further demonstrated an obnoxious and a superior attitude because of his rather high academic achievements.

This particular case, although far from being typical, is well illustrative of the subjective evaluation that would be involved in determining a grade for citizenship. John received a grade of F in citizenship because he significantly failed to qualify under the subjective components, application and consistency. John knew his work but never applied it and never demonstrated any consistency with respect to such application.

Case B

Mary, 10 years of age, came from a middle class family. Her grades were average. She demonstrated no great ability as an academician yet showed an ability to comprehend subject material of her course work. Observation indicated Mary to be an exceptionally talented and gregarious person. She took part in practically every social activity. She was well liked by her classmates and might be described as a "Popular girl."

Mary received a grade of A in citizenship primarily because observation revealed that she was consistently applying the evidences of her comprehension of social studies course work.

This case shows again the departure from classical dogma in that although being an average student in social studies. She manifested the ability of applying, and applying consistently, the factual information she obtained in her social studies exposure.

Case C

Peter, age 11 was an exceptionally poor student in every

respect. He came from an underprivileged family of 2 brothers and 4 sisters. This large family was crowded in a small development home where space was at a premium. His parents were irresponsible. Although he demonstrated mental capabilities in several instances, he was definitely unable to achieve satisfactory grades because of his adverse home environment. Peter, however, did show evidence of extreme degrees of leadership, popularity, and gregariousness in all of his contacts with fellow students.

This case is indicative of the other extreme where in a child unable to achieve satisfactory grades did excel in citizenship because of his consistency and application of factual material.

Preston suggests the following:

. . . . .ways in which teachers may collect information which is necessary for comprehensive evaluation of progress.

1. Observation of Pupil Behaviour.
2. Inspection of Children's work.
3. Study of Results of Teacher-Made Tests. Many teachers have found that it is better to have frequent short tests than infrequent long ones . . . . . . Objectives tests with true-or-false items or multiple-choice items are also suitable and should be occasionally given . . . . . Teacher-constructed tests should be corrected and returned to the pupils for discussion. Test results are properly kept as part of the pupil's record.
4. Study of Results of Standardized Tests.

From these cases and the previous discussion certain generalization can now be developed :

1. The principal purpose of the social studies is to develop better citizens.

2. Objective tests do not reveal citizenship qualities, they merely present evidence indicating memorizational ability.
3. Subjective observation is required in order to evaluate and determine citizenship qualities.
4. Subjective observation is directed toward determining the extent and degree in which a student consistently applies the overall philosophy of the social studies.
5. Evaluation skills can be developed in the teacher through exposure and observation of students in their play, classroom participation, and school environmental situation.

10
Improving Classroom Testing

In reviewing the 1965 Yearbook of the National Council for the Social Studies in search of practical solutions for improving classroom achievement tests, I was struck by the emphasis which author after author placed upon the essentiality of adequate planning.

First, planning necessitates the allocation of sufficient time for designing and constructing the test and sufficient time means a great deal of time. Thinking through objectives, composing (or even selecting) appropriate test items, assembling a proper number and balance of items into a draft instrument, reviewing the test, and putting it into final form are enormously time-consuming activities.

Second, planning involves a conscious determination of purpose — first in terms of the intended use of the test and then, but not less important, in terms of what is to be tested. The characteristics of tests intended for diagnosis, for measurement of growth, and for ranking students may be quite different but, without clear identification of intended use, the appropriate characteristics are not likely to be attained. Furthermore, a test, if it is to provide meaningful data, must offer evidence concerning some identifiable student behaviour. This behaviour in the social sciences will have two dimensions — one with reference to some body of subject-matter, the other with reference to kinds of learning, to the possession, for example, of knowledge of facts or sources, of understandings, of intellectual skills, or of critical thinking abilities. A good test must have validity (i.e., relevance to its intended purpose): and reliability (i.e., dependability in the sense that it does a good and consistent job of measurement). Obviously a test is unlikely to possess either of these qualities unless purposes have been thought through and defined in operational terms by the test maker.

Third, planning includes an evaluation of the intended takers of the test. Vocabulary employed and difficulty of items used must be appropriate to the students to be tested. An ideally good achievement test should give the best student an oppurtunity on demonstrate his superior attainment and allow the poorest student to accomplish something, yet to rank himself properly at the foot of the group. These things can occur only if the test is consciously adjusted to the capacity of its takers.

In addition to the emphasis on adequate planning, the Yearbook suggests strongly the desirability of exploiting the respective strengths of essay tests and objective tests by using both in the total testing program. The essay form offers the possibility of measuring qualities which are necessary attributes of the historian and the social scientist — knowledge understandings, and skills possessed in depth, the ability independently to organize material, and the capacity to communicate effectively in writing. The objective form can provide wider sampling, establish more nearly identical tasks as a basis for accurate ranking of students, and permit more uniform and impersonal grading.

Robert J. Solomon in his chapter on the essay test offers specific suggestions for the construction of essay examinations. He warns against the habitual use of the essay form to test the recall of memorized generalizations. If these are to be tested at all, the objective form can generally do the job better. So that the essay test may be an acceptable measuring device, Mr. Solomon urged, first, conscious structuring of the individual questions and of the whole test to provide a range of tasks as nearly as possible the same for every taker and, second, extreme care in grading. In essay tests, avoid the overworked direction, "discuss." Be specific; ask the students to list, define, illustrate, explain, defend, compare, differentiate, outline or summarize. Mr. Solomon also argues that there should be no choice permitted in the items to be answered. He points out that teachers seldom have evidence that alternative questions are of equal difficulty and that students are often incapable of determining for themselves on what items they will perform most creditably. Allowing students a choice of items really means presenting them with different tests. The grading of essay examinations should ideally involve (1) drafting model answers in advance to check on the clarity of the questions, the difficulty of expected answers, and the time it will take to respond; (2) reading a random sample of answers to check the level of responses and the presence of widespread unexpected interpretations; (3) attempting to avoid identifying papers with their authors; (4) grading question by question rather than paper by paper; (5) grading different questions in different sequences: and (6) periodically re-checking papers graded earlier to see that standards have not shifted during the grading process.

Finally, students should be informed of the ground rules in testing — the time available for the test, the weighting of various items, and whether spelling, grammar, and composition will be evaluated along with social science content.

Specific suggestions for the preparation of objective tests are to be found principally in Harry Berg's chapter on the objective test item and in my chapter on planning, assembling, and administering the objective test, but Henry Dyer's chapter on educational measurement. Hymen Chausow's on evaluation in critical thinking. Maxine Dunfee's on evaluation in the elementary school, and Robert Eoel's on using the results of measurement should not be ignored.

At the outset, it is important to recognize that the objective examination, will highly suitable for the testing of information recall, is by no means limited to this task. Incidentally, when recall is tested, it should be recall of significant information and broad concepts. The objective test, when properly constructed, can test for understandings, for skills, and for critical-thinking abilities. It can do this through the translation of knowledge into unfamiliar terms, the structuring of problem situations, and the presentation for interpretation of new material in the form of quotations, tables, graphs, maps, etc. Objective items may ask for identification of common elements: for causes, results, conclusions, illustrations, and examples; for the essential as distinguished from the incidental; for the central idea; for assumptions and implications; for the impartiality, relevance, and adequacy of facts in support of a generalization or conclusion; and for the difference between fact and opinion.

The form of objective items to be employed is of far less concern than the content of the items. There is much to be said, however, in favour in the four-response or five response, multiple-choice form. It is highly flexible in that it can be used either for discrete, self contained items or for groups of related items dependent upon quoted material. It also lends itself to use either in tests which seek the one "right" answer (often employed with factual material) or in those which seek the "best" answers (highly useful in dealing with understandings and skills).

To assure that the advantage of the objective test in setting the same task for all is really achieved, great care should be taken in the composition of the test items. Clarity and conciseness must be the watchwords. All responses (not merely the first) should follow logically and grammatically from the stem. Responses should parallel one another in phrasing and should, in general be of about the same length. "None of the above" may be an acceptable response when it makes a pertinent point. It cannot logically be used, however, with the "best answer" type of item. Also it should not be used, when other choices have already exhausted all *possible* alternatives. "All the above" may have the weakness of providing a clue to students who recognize that two of the other responses are true and, therefore, correctly choose the "all" answer even when they do not know that the remaining one or two answers are correct. This disadvantage can be obviated by specifying alternative combinations such as "1 and 2 above but not 3," "2 and 3 above, but not 1"or by presenting a series of labeled items in the stem (a, b, c etc.,) and offering varied combinations of these items in the responses.

To be as sure as possible that objective items are testing what the maker intends them to test, all items should be checked for unintended clues such as the use of specific determiners like "never" or "always" in wrong answers, the repetition of key words from the stem in the correct, but only in the correct, response, uniqueness of the correct response, and interlocking items in which the stem of one reveals the correct answer of another. Another way in which objective items may go astray and fail to test what is intended is through the presence of nonfunctioning content. Avoid introductory statements which contain intrinsically significant material but which are in fact unnecessary in answering the item in which they appear. Avoid giving so much information in the responses that different test takers may arrive at the correct answers on the basis of different kinds or levels of information or skill. Unless care is exercised, the laudable effort to make items more thought provoking may merely load them with nonfunctioning content and make them *appear* to test things which they really do not test.

Objective items should be recorded in such a way that they can be stored conveniently, filed by category for easy recovery, readily arranged and rearranged in the creation of a test, and broken up for re-use in a new context. These desiderata can be attained by the use of index cards. It is well to double space typed cards and to leave a place at the top of the card for category code, dates of use, and difficulty and discrimination data if these are calculated.

In the actual assembling of an objective test a number of matters should receive consideration.

First, the length of the test should be established. For achievement tests the objective should be to allow every student to consider every item. Since, if there is a wide range of ability and reading speed in the class, this may be impossible to attain and still not have some students finish far too soon, it is acceptable to adjust the length of the test so that between 80 and 90 percent of the takers will complete it.

Second, the difficulty level of the test should be considered. A good test should provide a wide range of difficulty in its items. Theoretically, the mean attained score should be near the middle of the available score range. In practice, when new items are being employed, the classroom teacher can do little more than use his best judgment, trying to avoid items which are patently too easy or too difficult for his students, classifying apparently acceptable items as "difficult," "moderate," or "easy" and placing on his test about an equal number of items from each of these three categories. The difficulty of items which have appeared on a test can be calculated and this information can be recorded for later use.

Third, the discrimination power of items must receive attention. Desirable items for a test are those which properly differentiate students who possess the traits being tested from those who do not Unfortunately the only practicable way to check the discriminating power of items is to use them on a test and to analyze their effectiveness. Even worse, the only easily available criterion against which to check these items is the total examination of which they are a part. The classroom teacher, therefore, must again rely in the first instance upon subjective judgment in selecting items that *appear* to be relevant to his test's defined purpose and that *seem* likely to discriminate well. He can, however, weed out from future use items which function poorly. This can be done by calculating a crude index of discrimination by methods suggested in chapter 9 and 10 of the Yearbook.

In planning and assembling an objective examination, it is good practice to employ a two-way table of test specifications to assure that the intended coverage of the test in terms of subject-matter and student behaviours is adhered to in execution. Examples of such tables appear in chapter 2 and 9 of the Yearbook. The first draft of a test should contain about 10 per cent more items than the final test, so that weak or unsatisfactory items may be withdrawn in the course or revision and review without necessitating the writing or selection of new items at the last moment. Items may be assembled at random, in order of increasing difficulty, or in terms of some logical arrangement by subject-matter. An effort to arrange a classroom test in order of item difficulty is likely to be frustrated by the inadequacy of data available. If the test is to be used by the students for review and study, the order of subject-matter often appears more desirable.

Once the test is assembled, it should be carefully read as a whole to detect clues arising from context, and a key should be made by actually taking the test. This key ought to be checked against the original keying of the items, and discrepancies should be accounted for and reconciled. In the final key, avoid patterned answers in which one position is habitually favoured, long consecutive runs of the correct response in the same position, and the consistent use of the same position for right answer. Finally, other qualified persons as many as possible — should review the examination, reading it critically and keying it independently. If this is impossible, the test should be laid aside for a time and then reviewed by the maker, who should approach it so far as possible as if it were someone else's creation.

An objective test should be designed and duplicated in such a way that each student may have a clear and conveniently arranged copy. Adequate directions, should appear at the beginning of the test, and the system of designating items and labeling responses should be unambiguous. There should be adequate indication of where and how answers are to be recorded. Meticulous proof reading of mimeograph stencils or ditto trial sheets is essential.

The grading of objective tests seems to raise fewer problems than the grading of essay examinations, since it can be done by machine if appropriate answer sheets are used, or almost mechanically by the teacher, a clerk, or by students. Yet certain problems do arise. One pertains to the weighting of items, another to the applying of a penalty for guessing. Concerning the first, the effect of item weighting can be gained, without the complexities ir scoring which this causes, by varying the number of items dealing with various behaviour traits or subject-matter areas. Concerning the second, the possibility of chance success on a five-response, multiple-choice item is small and, if everyone attempts all items, the application or nonapplication of a correction formula makes virtually no change in the rank order of test takers. It appears, therefore, that the ease of grading achieved by ignoring guessing and scoring simply the number of items right justifies this procedure.

Dr. Ebel suggests in the Yearbook that for an objective test there should be prepared a frequency distribution of scores, that the mean of the distribution and the standard deviation should be calculated, that letter grades might be assigned, that the reliability and the standard error of the score should be calculated, and that all these data should be reported and explained to the pupils. In the best of all possible worlds, where classroom teachers and their pupils had taken college courses in tests and measurements, this would certainly be helpful in creating better tests and making the testing process more meaningful and useful to students. In this imperfect world, I doubt its practicality.

There are, then, some suggestions in the 1965 Yearbook that most classroom teachers will probably not think it feasible to follow. There are many suggestions however, which are realistic for the use of the classroom teacher in dealing with the ever present and often frustrating task of effective teaching.

11

Strategies and Tactics in Elementary School Classrooms

During the 1970s there has been a rapid growth in the use of systematic observation to study teaching. Whereas the 1970 edition of *Mirrors for Behaviour* (Simon and Boyer, 1970) listed only two British instruments, a recently published anthology now shows that the number of home produced ones stands at 40 of which a sizable number are designed for use at primary school level (Galton, 1978).

One use of these techniques has been to describe styles of teaching (Eggleston, Galton and Jones, 1976; Galton, Simon and Croll, 1980). Teachers are sorted into groups whose characteristics are defined in terms of the relative frequency with which their members use the categories of the observation schedule. Used in this way the definition of teaching style differs from that used by other authors, notably in the report of the findings of the Lancaster study (Bennett, 1976). The purpose of this article is therefore to attempt a more precise definition of the term and to contrast the use of interaction analysis and questionnaires in providing descriptions of various teaching styles.

To illustrate points in the discussion, data from the ORACLE study (Simon and Galton, 1975) will be used, particularly data from the Teacher Record, an observation instrument developed in an earlier study (Boydell, 1974).

[Observational Research and Classroom Learning Evaluation, (ORACLE) is a five-year programme of research funded by the SSRC. Although this paper reflects the author's views, these have been developed over long periods of discussion with other members of the project team and their help, particularly that of Mr P. Croll, who undertook the data analysis, is most gratefully acknowledged.] This instrument clearly bears certain similarities to the Science Teacher Observation Schedule (STOS) which was developed to provide information about the range of teaching styles used in the new secondary science curricula (Eggleston, Galton and Jones, 1975). In developing their notion of teaching style these researchers laid stress on the distinction between teaching *strategy* and teaching *tactics* first put forward by Taba and Elzey (1964) and subsequently elaborated by Strasser (1967) in advancing a conceptual model of instruction. For Taba a strategy consists of a teacher's attempt to translate her aims into practice while tactics according to Strasser are the 'minute by minute exchanges' between a teacher and her pupils through which such strategies are implemented. The use of systematic observation with its precisely defined categories of teacher-pupil interaction provides an ideal means of examining such tactical exchanges. If these twin concepts are put into a practical context there appears to be three key strategic decisions that any teacher has to make when confronted with a new situation such as starting a fresh year with a new class. The first concerns the *organizational strategy,* how to manage the learning environment, the second the *curriculum strategy,* what to teach and the third the *instructional strategy,* how to teach it.

The organizational strategy is largely directed towards seeing that each pupil is allowed the maximum opportunity for learning. It will concern decision such as whether to teach the class as a whole or whether to organize group work or to provide for individualized instruction. When groups are used then there are decisions involving their composition (their size, balance between sexes, mixed ability, etc.). Such strategies are largely directed towards maintaining control and to producing an efficient working atmosphere. The curriculum strategy is concerned with the content and balance of the curriculum. At junior school stage, when separate subject teaching is preferred to an integrated approach, then the different degree of emphasis given to different subject areas will be reflected by the time-table. Within any subject area, however, there will be considerable room for each teacher to emphasize different aspects in her teaching. For example, a study by Ashton of primary teachers' aims showed that many teachers wished to give equal emphasis to applying basic skills to every-day practical situations as to using the four rules (Ashton *et al*, 1975). Such teachers would presumably give as much time to such activities as measuring and shopping games as they would to learning tables and doing formal sums.

The instructional strategy corresponds to what is often loosely called teaching methods and may include a combination of lecturing, demonstrating, class discussion, using work cards or project activity. For Taba the instructional strategy is the most important and she argues that the main function of teaching is to develop the pupils' capacity for thinking. Her instructional strategies are aimed at developing correct thinking in pupils and emphasise a questioning rather than a telling approach during class discussion. The ultimate aim is to allow pupils to manage their own learning so that they will make use of these questioning techniques even when the teacher is not present. It is clear that all three elements in the overall teaching strategy must be linked. A decision to engage in, for example, a discussion strategy would also involve decisions about organizational and curricular ones such as the nature of the groups and the selection and structuring of appropriate content in order to promote discussion among the pupils.

Teaching Tactics and Teaching Style

Once the lesson has begun the strategies have to be worked out by means of the exchanges between the teacher and her pupils — the teaching tactics. It is here suggested that each tactical exchange will seek to emphasise either an aspect of class *control,* the development of *social* and personal skills in the pupils or the pupils' *cognitive* development. Thus when a teacher asks a pupil a question 'two times two?' and receives the reply 'four' she is mainly concerned with a cognitive outcome but if she tells pupils, in a normal tone of voice, to 'carry on working and wait until I come to you' she is primarily exercising a management function designed to keep control of the teaching situation. The third type of tactic relating to social and personal development is not directly monitored by the observation schedules used in the ORACLE research, although it is reflected in some exchanges which give rise to teacher praise or criticism. However, because teachers who responded to the Ashton survey rated this a very important area it is being examined in a separate study as part of the ORACLE programme.

After a settling down period with the class a state of equilibrium is established where the teacher begins to make use of *a consistent set of tactics* and it is this which is here defined as her *teaching style.* According to Strasser the use of a set of tactics evolves mainly as a result of careful observation of pupil behaviour and less immediately because of previous knowledge about the pupils' attainment, but as the teacher and her pupils adjust to one another the latter's performance becomes an increasingly important factor in determining the relative success of the overall aims and strategy. Typically, however, researchers interested in teacher effectiveness have sought to define good and bad teaching mainly in terms of test results and to ignore pupil activity in the classroom. The ORACLE research programme is designed around the principle that a complete evaluation should concern itself with five elements in the teaching process listed in figure 1.

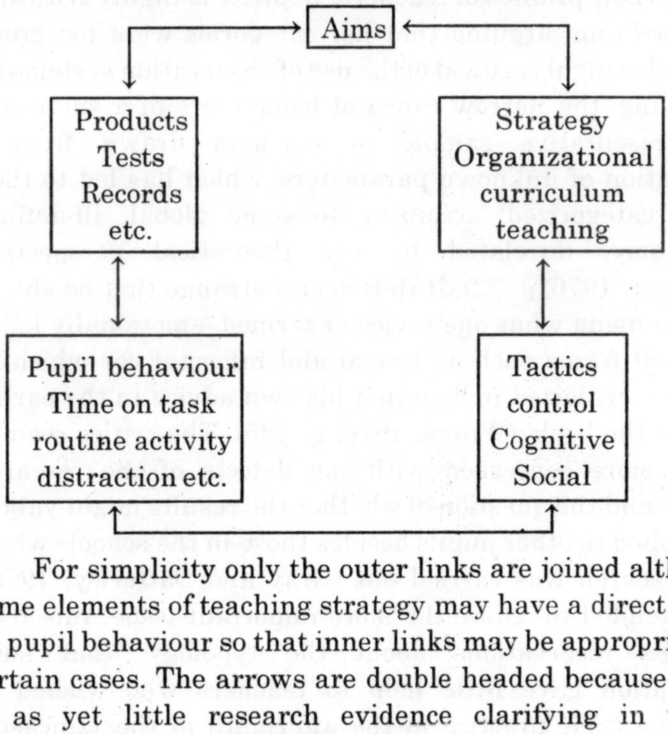

For simplicity only the outer links are joined although some elements of teaching strategy may have a direct effect on pupil behaviour so that inner links may be appropriate in certain cases. The arrows are double headed because there is as yet little research evidence clarifying in which direction these links should operate. ORACLE is one of the few studies to investigate whether there is even a relationship between certain kinds of teaching tactics and different types of pupil behaviour. Studies using naturalistic rather than experimental designs must introduce an element of replication if evidence is to be obtained about the direction of such relationships. Pupils in the ORACLE study will have been observed, in some cases, over three years. This will enable behaviour of pupils who move from one teacher to another of different style to be investigated.

The Use of Questionnaires to Study Teaching

Both Barker-Lunn (1970) and Bennett (1976) used questionnaires to obtain the information from which to derive their profiles of teachers. Bennett is highly critical of Barker-Lunn, arguing that her categories were too gross. He is also highly critical of the use of observation systems for observing 'the narrow range of behaviours of a small and unrepresentative sample of teachers drawn from a population of unknown parameters' which has led to their being categorized 'according to some global, ill-defined dichotomy, unrelated to any theoretical perspective'. (Bennett, 1976, p. 32). It thus seems strange that he should end up using what one reviewer termed 'emotionally laden catch-all terms such as formal and informal' for which he must be criticized in 'ignoring his own advice in the earlier part of the book' (Wragg, 1976, p. 285). The critics seemed much more concerned with the defects of the research design and the question of whether the results might validly be applied to other pupils besides those in the schools where the research was carried out (Gray and Satterley, 1976). They tended to ignore the more important issue, raised by Wragg's reservations about the typology, that such description gave little help to teachers who wished to examine their practice in the aftermath of the Lancaster study.

It could be argued, however, that this weakness derives directly from the use of questionnaires which require an individual to answer each item by selecting one response from a limited number of mutually exclusive categories. This means, for example, that on the Bennett's questionnaire teachers who gave tests every fortnight and who answered the question 'Do you give pupils an arithmetic test at least once a week?' would be classified as not giving regular tests alongside those teachers who never tested at all.

More importantly, certain results appear illogical in that some individuals were classified both as separate subject teachers and also as favouring an integrated subject approach. This comes about because of the way in which the data were collected and subsequently analyzed. Teachers were asked to estimate how much of a 25 hour working week they devoted to academic subjects taught separately, integrated subjects and aesthetic subjects, the latter including PE and games. The means on each of the categories were calculated and teachers were classified either as above or below the mean on each of the three dimensions. Because the amount of time given to aesthetics was dependent on that allocated to single subject and integrated subject teaching it was omitted from the analysis, but teachers who gave little attention to such things as art, music and drama could easily find themselves 'above average' on both single subject and integrated subject; teaching.

Even if teachers could recognize themselves within these formal - informal labels the descriptions provided give little guidance about what they might do or say to pupils during lessons. It was left to Wragg (1978) to try to identify, through observation, such practices in the most successful of all Bennett's teachers, who used the informal style. In so doing he gives support to the view that descriptions based on observation are likely to make better sense to teachers since they highlight the activities on which those who differ in their effectiveness, differ in their treatment of pupils. Such descriptions are at the tactical rather than the strategic level.

Only observational studies can supply such information. At their best questionnaires tell us about a teacher's aims and offer global descriptions of teaching in terms of its strategies. Both Barker-Lunn's and Bennett's descriptions of teaching style, based as they were on questionnaire data, provide for the most part information about organizational and curricular strategies. In placing such emphasis on the teacher's management function Bennett would appear to reject the model of teaching proposed here and to support the views advanced by Harnischfeger and Wiley (1975, 1978) who dispute the notion that teaching behaviour directly influences pupils achievement. They argue instead that 'active learning time', the use a pupil makes of opportunities to study a given content, is the most important indicator of his progress. In the Lancaster study a certain amount of observation took place but it was only directed at the pupils and not at the teachers. The success of the formal style was attributed to the organizational strategies that these teachers adopted (working in silence, class teaching, giving rewards, etc.) which resulted in their pupils spending more time on their work (Bennett, 1978).

Instruments Used and Method of Analysis

To examine the relationship between strategy and tactics the process data from the 58 teachers observed during the first year of the ORACLE study were supplemented by additional sources of information. These are shown in Table 1A session summary sheet (SI) and a daily summary sheet (S2) were completed at the end of each observation session and at the end of the day respectively. They concern the physical layout of the classroom, seating arrangements, an outline of the curricular activity and, where available, a class time-table. A special grouping instrument was also completed giving detailed information about the grouping policy and its rationale. The teacher's questionnaire which was collected by the observers towards the end of the year reflected aspects of organizational and curricular strategies covered by both Barker-Lunn and Bennett but not dealt with in the summary sheets or the grouping instrument. Finally the observers were asked to write a descriptive account after each visit which recorded their general impressions of the classroom climate, the teaching methods and the relationships within the classroom. The use of these four sets of data enabled each teacher to be classified on each of the 19 dimensions used by Bennett for his teaching typology.

The main categories of the observation instrument, the Teacher Record, are shown in Table 2. Full details of the instrument can be found elsewhere (Galton *et al*, 1980). Its purpose was to record the various kinds of contact which the teacher engaged in with her pupils using a 25 second time-sampling unit. At each signal the observer noted down different aspects of these interactions. He first indicated the type of *conversation* or the nature of the *silent interaction* taking place. The silent interaction categories were included to show when the teacher was *gesturing, showing* by writing or demonstrating on the blackboard, *marking* pupils work in their presence, *waiting* for the class to settle, reading a *story* or listening to a pupil *reading* aloud. To deal with cases where the observer had difficulty in recording the activities two further categories, *not observed* and *not coded* were available. If no interaction was taking place then one of four categories under this heading was coded. These covered such events as visits from other teachers or

Table 1. Instruments used in data collection (Autumn 1976-Summer 1977)

Title	When completed	Focus
Pupil record (PR)	Each target pupil was observed once during each of the six observation sessions per term. Oservations were made in the Autumn, Spring and Summer terms. (1976-1977)	Pupil's activities and interactions with other pupils and adults
Teacher record (TR)	Each teacher was observed once during each of the six observation sessions per term, Observations were made in Autumn, Spring and Summer terms (1976-1977)	Teacher questions and statements, silent interaction, no interaction and the audience, its composition and curricular activity
Session summary	This was completed at the end of each observation Therefore, six were colleced each term (Autumn, Spring and Summer, (1976-1977)	Physical layout of the classroom, seating of all pupils; outline of curricular contents and methods used; apparatus, resources, etc. and incidents. Order and time of observations.
Daily summary (sheet (S2)	This was completed at the end of each day, therefore, three were collected each term (Autumn, Spring and Summer, 1976-1977)	Calss time-table, and outline of organization to include all activities whether observed or not
Impressionistic account (S3)	This was completed for each class, once a term, at the end of the six observation sessions (Autumn term 1976, Spring term 1977)	Prose account of the impressions of the observer as regards the teacher, classroom climate, teching methods, etc.
Grouping instrument (GI)	This was completed for each class in the Summer term 1977	Physical layout, grouping policy and rationale
Teacher's questionnaire (TQ)	This was completed for each class in the Summer term 1977.	Classroom management/ organiztion similar to Bennett's (1976) survey

parents *(adult interaction)* and from pupils from other classes *(visiting pupil), not interacting* while silently monitoring or going out *of room* for some purpose or other. Finally the observer coded the type of the teacher *audience* (class, group or individual) its *composition* and certain features of the curricular *activity* of the child or children with whom the teacher was interacting.

Table 2. The observation categories of the teacher record

CONVERSATION		
	Questions	
	Task	
	Q1	Recalling facts
	Q2	Offering ideas, solutions (closed)
	Q3	Offering ideas, solutions (open)
	Task supervision	
	Q4	Referring to task supervision
	Routine	
	Q5	Referring to routine matter
	Statements	
	Task	
	S1	Of facts
	S2	Of ideas, problems
	Task supervision	
	S3	Telling child what to do
	S4	Praising work of effort
	S5	Feedback on work or effort
	Routine	
	S6	Providing information, directions
	S7	Providing feedback
	S8	Of critical control
	S9	Of small talk

SILENCE

Silent interaction
Gesturing
Showing
Marking
Waiting
Story
Reading
Not observed
Not coded
No interaction
Adult interaction
Visiting pupil
Not interacting
Out of room
Audience
Composition
Activity

A second instrument, the Pupil Record (Boydell, 1975) was also used in the study but does not concern us here. Teachers and pupils were alternatively observed, each teacher receiving twenty minutes observation time per session. There were two sessions a day and each class received a visit lasting three days each term throughout the year. The reliability of the instrument had been amply demonstrated previously (Boydell, 1974) but a further trial with team of observers in live classrooms gave average values on the main variables of 0.76 using the Scott (1955) coefficient. These figures were based on the individual coding of specific time units whereas in the study the total number of tallies was aggregated for each category in order to determine the teaching style. It is generally accepted that reliabilities of this order are satisfactory for this type of analysis. In some cases it also proved possible to join categories together during the aggregation procedure thus increasing the overall reliability of the combination.

To identify teaching styles a cluster analysis was carried out using the 20 interaction variables (excluding the categories *not observed* and *not listed)and* the two audience categories *class interaction and group interaction*. The third audience category *individual interaction* was not included because it was dependent on the levels of the other two. The 're-location' procedure developed for the PMMD package (Youngman, 1975) was used which is a modified version of Wishart's Clustan system of computer programmes (Wishart, 1969) and this gave a stable four cluster solution. The analysis was replicated on two further occasions, first, to check that using a different initial random allocation made no difference to the result and, second, to test the effect of excluding the two audience categories. This was done because the audience variables are concerned more with the organizational strategy rather than with teaching style and it was feared that the former might exert a disproportionate influence and mask the variation in the use of tactics by different teachers. However, even with the audience categories omitted a similar solution to the one obtained in the fuller analysis still emerged. This was of the utmost importance in showing that the interaction categories, indicative of tactical decisions, rather than organizational strategies were the major source of differentiation between the clusters, although as will be seen the two were closely related.

Characteristics of Teaching Styles

The main characteristics of the four cluster solution of the Teacher Record data are given in Table 3. Their most obvious feature relates to the different use made of the audience categories but, as has been pointed out, this aspect of organizational strategy cannot be the major determinant of the clusters since the solution remained stable even when the audience categories were omitted from the analysis. In terms of the total amount of teacher - pupil interaction taking place, all four groups showed similar patterns in that they were actively involved on more than three-quarters of the occasions when observations were made. The manner in which this attention was distributed varied considerably but it would be wrong simply to describe teachers in cluster 1, for example, as 'individualized' and those in cluster 2 as 'class oriented' since the variation between these groups on the kinds of interactions which represent teaching tactics is highly significant. It is this variation which can be used to provide descriptions of each teaching style.

Table 3. Cluster characteristics as percentage of total observations

		1 Individual monitors	2 Class enquirers	3 Group instructors	4 Style changer
Questions	Q1 Recalling facts	3.9	4.1	2.4	3.4
	Q2 Solution (closed)	1.1	3.3	2.0	2.4
	Q3 Solution (open)	0.3	1.0	0.9	0.6
	All task questions	5.3	8.4	5.3	6.4
	Q4 Task supervision	2.9	4.1	3.2	4.5
	Q5 Routine	1.3	2.2	1.5	2.0
	All other questions	4.2	6.3	4.7	6.5
Statements	S1 Of facts	5.6	8.0	11.9	6.0
	S2 Of ideas	2.1	4.2	1.0	2.6
	All task statements	7.7	12.2	12.9	8.6
Task supervision:	S3 Telling	15.8	11.2	11.6	11.8
	S4 Praising	1.0	1.3	0.6	1.1
	S5 Feedback	8.7	10.9	15.9	8.7
Routine:	S6 Information	5.6	7.0	6.7	6.8
	S7 Feedback	1.8	2.3	2.3	2.0
	S8 Critical control	2.0	1.5	2.4	2.6
	S9 Small talk	1.3	1.7	0.6	1.4
	All other statements	36.2	35.9	40.1	34.4

		1	2	3	4
Silent interaction					
Gesturing		1.8	0.9	3.7	1.8
	Showing	2.4	3.3	2.0	2.6
	Marking	16.4	5.7	7.4	9.4
	Waiting	1.7	1.6	2.1	2.0
	Story	0.6	1.8	1.0	0.7
	Reading	3.0	3.4	2.2	3.8
	All other interactions	25.9	16.7	18.4	20.3
Audience	Individual	66.9	42.5	52.3	55.3
	Group	5.5	5.8	17.7	6.3
	Class	6.9	31.2	11.4	14.6

Style 1

This group accounted for 22.4 per cent of the sample and was characterized by the low level of questioning and the high level of silent interaction. The teachers engaged in a large number of short-lived interactions which were usually concerned with telling pupils what to do (task supervision S3). The general impression gained, from a variety of accounts provided by the observers, was of pupils working mainly on individual tasks with teachers under a considerable amount of pressure. The observers describe some teachers moving rapidly from table to table but others sitting at their desks with pupils queuing up either for information or for some clarification of the instructions in the text-book or worksheet. The pupil -adult categories on the Pupil Record indicate that most of these interactions were brief. Some pupils wished to know how to spell a word, others wanted to know whether they should go on to the next exercise. Any attempt by the teacher at prolonged interaction with a pupil was usually prevented by the pressures resulting from the demands of the other pupils and from her concern to keep waiting time to a minimum.

Within such a complex organization the task of monitoring the pupils' work takes on a high priority. It is important not only to correct books but also to record progress so that where pupils are involved in planning their own time-tables regular checks can be carried out to see if each has fulfilled his quota. There was thus a very high level of interaction concerned with marking. Under the ground rules of the observation schedule, marking consists of the teacher giving feedback by writing corrections on pupil's work rather than by making oral comments. It is this particular characteristic which suggests that Style 1 should be labelled as *individual monitors*.

Style 2

This group comprised 15.5 per cent of the sample and was defined by the emphasis given to questioning, particularly questions relating to task work. The level of statements made was also relatively high which suggested, in keeping with the amount of class teaching, that much of the learning was 'teacher managed'. However, when examining the sub-categories of teacher talk it can be seen that much of the conversation related to the higher cognitive levels. Although the level of cognitive discourse in junior school classrooms appears, for the most part, to be concerned with the transmission of information, the teachers under Style 2 used a much higher proportion of both closed and open questions (Q2, Q3) and made more statements of ideas and problems (S2) than did the remaining groups.

The picture which came from the observers' impressionistic accounts was of teachers who introduced new topics to the whole class and then engaged in question and answer routines with individual pupils, reinforced by means of verbal feedback on their work. Because of this emphasis on problem solving, coupled with teacher control of these activities by means of class teaching, it seems apt to describe this group of teachers as engaging in *class directed enquiry*.

Style 3

This cluster consists of 12.1 per cent of the teachers and was in many ways the most interesting. The amount of group interaction was, on average, three times as high as for the rest of the sample. The decrease in time given over to individual attention allowed the teacher to engage in considerably more teacher directed interaction (questioning and stating) than, for example, teachers in Style 1. The main emphasis, however, was on making statements of fact rather than the presentation of ideas. This was coupled with a high level of verbal feedback and gesturing. Presumably, and the observer's descriptions tend to confirm this, these teachers preferred to structure the work of the group carefully before allowing them to engage in discussion among themselves. Hence there was an emphasis on giving information (SI) and, once the group began to interact, on returning to re-join the discussion and provide verbal feedback on the pupils' ideas and solutions to problems. Set against the general low level of cognitive questioning these teachers did nevertheless engage in above average amounts of open questioning. This suggests that they allowed the groups of pupils to come up with alternative answers to problems and did not always insist on their being the one correct answer. Such teachers appear to come closest in adopting the grouping strategy suggested by Plowden for coping with large sized classes. Although there was evidence for some less directed enquiry since these teachers also tended to ask more open questions the main emphasis must be placed on the information aspects of their teaching. Consequently this group might be thought of as *group instructors.*

Style 4

Fifty per cent of the sample came within this cluster. It

appears to be a mixture of the other three since in the audience category, for example, these teachers had the second highest levels of individual, group and class interaction, even given that some of these differences are slight. They did ask the highest number of questions relating to task supervision (Q4), made more statements of critical control (S8) and heard more pupils read than did teachers in other styles but these features were not associated exclusively with one particular remaining cluster. Style 2, the *class directed enquirers,* also engaged in task supervision questions and reading while Style 1 teachers, the *individual monitors,* showed a similar need for an element of critical control.

Although overall there was considerable variation in the amount of higher order cognitive interactions between styles, when this was broken down between class and individual attention, then it appears that there is something about class teaching which is particularly conducive to such activity. For example, the individual monitors who have the lowest amount overall of this type of interaction nevertheless contrived to engage in 16.7 per cent of it when in conversation with the whole class. For the group instructors (Style 3) the corresponding figure is 19.5 per cent. Thus the use of certain types of tactics seems closely related to different organizational strategies and the impressionistic accounts for this group of teachers confirm that they all in one way or another make changes in their organization during the year. Some made *infrequent* changes shifting from a class to a more individualized approach as the year progressed. Others set up activity areas and the pupils *rotated* from one table to the next at regular intervals. The third sub-group carried *out frequent* changes which in many cases seemed unplanned, often in reaction to some undesired pupil behaviour. Thus one teacher, Miss S., tended to move swiftly to class activities at any time when the general level of 'busyness' dropped and the volume of noise rose to any marked degree. This additional evidence lends support to the description of the teachers in cluster 4 as *style changers where the* emphasis on certain sets of tactics varies according to the preferred pattern of organization at any time.

Organizational Strategies and Teaching Styles

These links between organizational strategy and teaching styles are interesting and in some ways surprising. The Plowden Report suggests the use of teaching methods which imply open-ended questioning tactics associated with pupil management of the learning environemtn using an integrated subject matter approach. The ORACLE study can find little evidence for this combination of tactics and strategy. At the other end of the scale those critics who argued that traditional standards have fallen because in the new informally organized classrooms teachers were taking to the extreme the belief that 'children should not be told anything but must find out for themselves' (Cox and Dyson, 1969), appear to have exaggerated their fears. As far as progressivism in its purest form is concerned it has not so much as failed as has yet to be tried.

Both Barker-Lunn and Bennett, however, also showed that the use of class teaching was strongly associated with certain groups in their respective typologies of teaching. Barker-Lunn's type 2 teachers, the more traditional, made more use of class teaching but they also believed in streaming, were less tolerant of noise and talking, showed less interest in the work of the slow child and had favourable attitudes to physical punishment (Barker-Lunn, 1970, pp. 52-53). In Bennett's (1976, p. 47) study the most extreme formal group were portrayed as follows:

an extreme group in a number of respects. None favour an integrated approach. Subjects are taught separately by class teaching and individual work. None allow pupils choice of seating, and every teacher curbs movement and talk. These teachers are above average on assessment and procedures (weekly testing) and extrinsic motivation (awarding stars and grades) predominates.

If similarities do exist then the *class enquirers* (Style 2) who do most class teaching should exhibit the characteristics of Bennett's formal teachers while the *individual monitors* (Style 1) should have more in common with his informal group (type 1). The Bennett typology was based upon nineteen variables. For this comparison the five which described variations in the use of class, group or individual teaching were excluded. Data about the remaining fourteen variables was collected for ORACLE teachers in a variety of ways. The observers completed the teaching questionnaire, giving such information as whether there were weekly tests in mathematics and spelling, whether pupils were given a choice where to sit, whether the class were expected to work in silence and so on. From the observer records, the session and daily summary sheets (S1 and S2), it was possible to estimate the percentage of single subject and integrated subject teaching.

The results were then analyzed in exactly the same way as in Bennett's original research. For example, the data on single subject teaching were dichotomised to differentiate between teachers who were above and below the mean of this variable. The same procedure was used for integrated subject teaching. As with the Lancaster teachers, because aesthetic subjects were given so little time, some of the ORACLE sample were 'above average' on both 'single' and 'integrated' subject teaching.

The data are presented in Table 4. For comparison the figures for Bennett's formal and informal types are included. In general the differences between the *individual monitors* and the *class enquirers* were less marked than those between the teachers in the Lancaster study. Only on two of the variables, allowing *choice of seats* and *freedom of movement* was the trend almost as extreme. Seventy-five per cent of the *individual monitors* insisted on quiet. Forty-one and 50 per cent respectively gave weekly tests in arithmetic and spelling compared to 9 and 23 per cent of the informal teachers. Far fewer *class enquirers* gave homework, awarded marks or stars, and smacked pupils than did the formal teachers. On three of the key items, held by supporters of traditional methods to be essential components of 'good' teaching, the differences were completely eliminated or actually reversed. *Class enquirers* were equally likely to use the same balance of integrated and single subject teaching as the *individual monitors* and an equally large percentage were against seating by ability within the class. The *individual monitors* were more likely to discipline pupils by sending them out of the classroom. This latter finding conflicts with Barker-Lunn's claim that teachers who favoured less 'traditional' methods were likely to be more permissive (Barker-Lunn, 1970, p. 55).

One further important finding from the Barker-Lunn study was that the teachers using the traditional approach (type 2) were less interested in the slow child. In this present study the two teachers who were most typical of the *class enquirers,* in that their use of the categories of the Teacher Record was closest to the means of the cluster profile, both told observers that they used class teaching to gain more time for dealing with the slow learners. In each case the observers commented that both classes were 'pleasant places to be in' where the teachers were observed to 'interact for lengthy periods with individual children who were experiencing difficulties with the work'.

Table 4. Percentage of teachers in each teaching style who were above average on 'formal - informal' characteristics

	Individual monitors	*Class enquirers*	*Bennett informal*	*Bennett formal*
Choice of seats	67	22	63	0
Seating by ability	25	22	14	50
Free movement	92	11	51	0
Quiet	75	89	31	100
Out of school visits	8	0	51	42
Homework	8	0	9	56
Marks	0	11	3	97
Stars	17	44	9	75
Arithmetic tests	41	78	9	81
Spelling tests	50	100	23	92
Children smacked	33	44	34	58
Sent from room	33	11	11	11
Single subjects	66	67	20	92
Integrated subjects	41	44	97	0

Thus none of the ORACLE teaching styles can be identified with the extremes of the formal - informal dichotomy. This leads to an alternative suggestion as to why the formal group, who emphasised class teaching, were more successful. Possibly, as did the ORACLE class teachers, they engaged in more higher level cognitive interactions. Since the Lancaster study ignored these kinds of teaching variables when collecting data it is impossible to test out this hypothesis directly. Initial analysis of the ORACLE *product* data indicates that the *class directed enquiry* teachers were successful particularly in mathematics but less so with less able pupils than were a sub-group of the style changers who engaged in even higher levels of this type of intellectual transaction.

There is, however, support for other conclusions from

the Bennett study. In particular, the use of individualized instruction at the expense of almost any other type of classroom organization is shown to create severe problems in that such teachers are so taken up with planning and running this complex learning environment that they have little time for engaging in any kind of direct teaching with their pupils. This leaves them with very difficult decisions as to which pupils to ignore and which to interact with. Some of the impressionistic accounts suggest that in classes where the teacher sits at the desk and silently marks books, the bright and slower pupils get extra attention: the bright ones because they finish work quickly and come out for a fresh task while the slower pupils, if they are disruptive, are called out by the teacher so that she can find out 'what they are doing'. It may be, therefore, that quieter average pupils who get on with their work lose out in this situation.

One alternative for overcoming these difficulties, where some class teaching is either impracticable or goes against the teacher's inclination, would be to make more use of group work. In the ORACLE study group work was taken to mean pupils working *cooperatively* on a *common task*. This differs from the more usual interpretation which in most cases means nothing more than pupils sitting at the same table engaged in their own separate tasks in a related subject area. In the absence of a common task the teacher has very few opportunities to talk with the group as a whole so that the amount of attention which each pupil can hope to receive must remain low. Considerably more detailed analysis needs to be carried out before the full effects of changing strategy in this way can be known. The ORACLE programme is a longitudinal study in which some teachers and their pupils will have been observed for three years so that the effect of changing teaching style can be investigated. Hopefully this will add a little to our knowledge and understanding of teaching. In reaching towards this understanding, the breakdown of the teaching process into strategy and tactics seems to provide a meaningful descriptive model. This should be of use, not only to the researcher, but also to those attempting to improve current practice in both the initial training and in-service fields.

References

Ashton, P. *et al,* (1975) *The Aims of Primary Education: A Study of Teachers' Opinions* Schools Council Research Series, London, Macmillan Education.

Barker-Lunn, L.J.C. (1970) *Streaming in the Primary School* Slough, NFER, pp. 26-27, 55, 58, 81.

Bennett, N. (1976) *Teaching Style and Pupil Progress* London, Open Books.

Bennett, N. (1978) 'Recent research on teaching: A dream, a belief, and a model' *British Journal of Educational Psychology* 48, pp. 127-147.

Boydell, D. (1974) 'Teacher-pupil contact in junior classrooms' *British Journal of Educational Psychology* 44, pp. 313-318.

Boydell, D. (1975) Pupil behaviour in junior classrooms, *British Journal of Educational Psychology* 45, pp. 122-129.

Cox, C. and Dyson, A. (Eds) (1969) *Black Paper Two: The Crisis in Education* Critical Quarterly Society,

Eggleston, J.F., Galton, M.J. and Jones, M.E. (1975) *A Science Teaching Observation Schedule* Schools Council Research Series, London, Macmillan Education.

Eggleston, J.F., Galton, M.J. and Jones, M.E. (1976) *Processes and Products of Science Teaching* Schools Council Research Series, London, Macmillan Education.

Galton, M., Simon, B. and Croll, P. (1980) *Inside the Primary Classroom* London, Routledge and Kegan Paul.

Galton, M.J. (1978) *British Mirrors: A Collection of Classroom Observation Systems* School of Education, University of Leicester.

Gray, J. and Satterly, D. (1976) 'A chapter of errors: Teaching styles and pupil progress in retrospect' *Educational Research* 19, pp. 45-56,

Harnischfeger, A. and Wiley, D. (1975) 'Teaching/learning processes in elementary schools: A synoptic view' *Studies of Education Processes* No. 9, University of Chicago.

Harnischfeger, A. and Wiley, D. (1978) 'Conceptual issues in models of school learning' *Journal of Curriculum Studies* 10, pp. 215-231.

Scott, W.A. (1955) 'Reliability of content analysis: The case of nominal coding' *Public Opinion Quarterly* 19, pp. 321-325.

Simon, A. and Boyer, E.G. (Eds) (1970) *Mirrors for Behaviour II: An Anthology of Observation Instruments* Research for Better Schools Inc., Philadelphia.

Simon, B. and Galton, M.J. (1975) *Observational Research and Classroom Learning Evaluation* (ORACLE) — an SSRC Programme, University of Leicester.

Strasser, B. (1967) 'A conceptual model of instruction' *Journal of Teacher Education* 18, pp. 63-74.

Taba, H. and ELZEY, F.F. (1964) 'Teaching strategies and thought processes' *Teacher College Record* 65, pp. "524-534.

Wishart, D. (1969) *Clustan 1A: User Manual* University of St Andrews Computing Laboratories, Fife, Scotland.

Wragg, E.G. (1976) 'The Lancaster study: Its implications for teacher training' *British Journal of Teacher Education 2,* pp. 281-290.

Wragg, E.G. (1978) 'A suitable case for imitation' *Times Educational Supplement,* 15 September, p. 18.

Youngman, M. (1975) *Programmed Methods for Multivariate Data* (PMMD), Version 4, University of Nottingham, School of Education, Nottingham.

12

Multiple Realities and their Reproduction in Infants' Classrooms

A number of studies in the sociology of education have drawn upon the social phenomenology of Alfred Schutz, which stresses the primacy of everyday life as the immediate and most important social reality. The purpose of this paper is to report the application of a relatively neglected aspect of Schutz's work, the concept of multiple realities, in relation to some of the teaching-learning processes in infants' classrooms, and to consider its general usefulness in the analysis of the curriculum.

The Research

The research reported here was part of a study of three large infants' schools (King, 1978) which used an action approach derived from Weber (one of the starting points for Schutz's theories), who defined social action as, 'all human behaviour when and insofar as the acting individual attaches subjective meaning to it' (Weber, trans. 1947). Our primary task was to to interpret the meanings teachers assigned to their actions in the classroom. This was attempted by long-term observations and follow-up interviews.

Our basic interpretation, which, following Schutz's postulate of adequacy (Schutz, 1953) was broadly confirmed by the teachers, was that their actions in the classroom were related to their definitions of the nature of young children and their education. These took the form of what Berger and Luckmann (1971) call recipes, that is, accepted ways of doing things. In Weberian terms they were institutionalized ideologies, taken for granted and given the status of the truth (Eldridge, 1971). The principal elements were: developmentalism, individualism, play as learning and childhood innocence, all familiar as the child-centred progressive ideology, as propagated by the Plowden Report (1967).

The concept of innocence was the most important in relation to the report that follows. There were two aspects to this. First, young children although capable of being naughty, were not necessarily judged as being naughty in intention. This was shown very clearly in the oblique methods of social control used by the teachers, who would say, 'Someone's being silly', rather than make a direct rebuke, and in their professional equanimity when children, for example, split paints for the fourth time or wet their pants.

Innocence also refers to the way children were protected from what their teachers defined as harmful or upsetting aspects of the outside world. This was shown very clearly in their management of the knowledge of death. When guinea pigs became old they were taken away from school by the teachers, partly because they tended to get snappy, but also to prevent their deaths being witnessed by the children. A gerbil in a cage outside a classroom died just as afternoon school was finishing. A girl noticed its death throes and asked, 'What's wrong with it?' His teacher replied, 'Oh nothing to worry about, you can go home now'. Later she said to me, 'Thank goodness they didn't see it'.

The Multiple Realities of Story Worlds

The main emphasis in the research was the teacher's creation of the everyday world of the classroom, but other worlds were also presented to the children. When they read the books provided or had books read to them by their teachers they were given access to a number of story worlds. The teachers had not written these books but in many cases they had chosen them, and so implicitly, and sometimes explicitly, approved of their contents. This is confirmed in their disapproving certain other kinds of books. When children brought annuals they had received as Christmas presents to school their teachers showed a polite but unenthusiastic interest and never read from them at story time. Some expressed a rather inchoate abhorrence of these books which was often extended to comics.

The most obvious of the approved story worlds were those in the introductory reading books. At one school the *Ladybird* series was in use. A content analysis, including the illustrations, shows why they were approved, since the story world created by the author is in many ways similar to the classroom world that the teachers attempted to create.

The principal characters of the first nine books are Peter and Jane. They are described and illustrated as infants' teachers ideally defined young children to be. They are invariably happy, having 'fun' and 'liking' everything. Of the 429 scenes identifiable in these books twenty-nine per cent show active or imaginative play. Peter and Jane play happily together with their friends, taking turns, sharing sweets and cakes, and are never naughty. They are moderately adventurous but are careful to do nothing dangerous. They are kind and caring towards animals and other children, taking presents to a friend in hospital and even their own toys for some less fortunate patients. At home they are keen to help, and are always careful to tidy up their toys before going to bed.

Peter and Jane go to school and are seen with their teachers who are talking to or supervising small groups of children, giving them interesting things to do or showing them something in a *Ladybird* book. However, Peter and Jane are more often seen outside school, but engaged in teacher-approved activities in contexts similar to those provided in the classroom. They have their own dressing-up box and a cupboard full of toys. They have no sandpit or water tray but they splash and play in the nearby stream and are taken on trips to the seaside. They have no playground or climbing frame but they play in the grassy garden and build Indian camps and tree houses. The house they live in is their Wendy house and Jane does 'real' cooking in her mother's kitchen. Shopping is done in 'real' shops not the toy shops of the classroom.

The adults in Peter and Jane's world are smiling, kind and helpful. Mother is the more prominent parent who, like the infants' teacher, talks and plays with them. The bedtime story is parallelled by story time at the end of the school day, followed by teacher tucking the children into their coats instead of their beds until tomorrow morning.

The reading scheme used in another of the three schools was the *Gay Way* series. The books of this series, colour coded from red to orange, present three fairly distinct story worlds; a 'real' world of human beings, an animal-humanoid world, and the traditional story world, each, in the terms of Alfred Schutz (1967) 'a finite province of meaning'. Schutz pointed out that human beings have the capacity for living in quite different worlds of meaning. We assign different significances to an accident in the street outside our house, to a similar event on the television news, or reported in a newspaper, or part of the events in a play or novel. Schutz called these worlds of meaning multiple-realities, the most intense, the paramount reality being that of everyday life. In school this is the everyday life of the classroom. The realities of the three story worlds of the *Gay Way* series corresponded in different degrees to the teachers' definition of the classroom situation, but in ways that were consistent with their child-centred ideologies.

The *'real' world of human beings* is very similar to Peter and Jane's world. Ken, Pat and Pipkin (a girl) also live in the country and own pets they care for. They are happy, kind, co-operative and affectionate children, playing and having fun with games similar to those of Peter and Jane. The adults, too, are kindly and helpful. There is no evil in this world, and when things go wrong, as when Pipkin's doll falls out of the train window, someone puts it right, as, without a reproach, her mother recovers the doll.

The animals in the 'real' world of human beings do not talk to one another or to people, as they do in the *animal-humanoid world*. Although not dressed as humans they are drawn in an anthropomorphic way. The dominant theme of the stories is the need for security. The animals are constantly looking for, and making homes, sometimes needing to co-operate to accomplish this. Many stories of lost kittens, chicks and baby rabbits end in their finding their mothers (fathers are conspicuously absent). Animals can be naughty. In the first book the pig excluded from the tin-pot house squashes it by sitting on it. But, usually naughtiness and carelessness have their consequences; unlatched gates and unlocked doors lead to unpleasant experiences. Some animals are quite malevolent, especially the fox. Death occurs in this world. The black beetle drowns in the stew, a consequence of his foolishness in stirring it with a small spoon. His companion, the ant, briefly grieves for him, but is soon consoled by the appearance of another beetle. In the *Mouse and the Flea,* jokes get out of hand leading to the mouse jumping out of his skin and losing his back legs and tail.

The presentation of the animal-humanoid world as a reality distanced from that of the 'real' world, mitigates the presumed effects that descriptions of macabre mutilations, evil and death may have upon the vulnerable innocence of children. Such things are presumed less 'real', and therefore less upsetting than they would be in the world of Pipkin.

In the 'real' world of humans, conventional reality is largely preserved. In the animal-humanoid world it is modified by the replacement of humans by animals. Human beings, when they rarely appear, do not communicate with animals. In the *traditional story world* humans, animals, plants and objects speak to one another. Magic transformations are possible. Events are unpredictable. They are not always the logical consequences of actions but are due to luck, spells or bad fortune.

The 'real' world of Pipkin is wholly good, and, apart from the bad foxes and trolls, the animal-humanoid is also good; misfortune only follows foolishness. In the traditional story world all reality is rather slippery, and morality is less clearly defined. A common theme, as in *The Animals' Winter Hut,* is the necessity to stick together in a wicked and unpredictable world. The child-reader is protected from harm by the distancing of this story world away from the everyday life idealized in the 'real' world stories. The 'unreality' of magic, of talking animals and objects are part of this, and the humans are not dressed in contemporary styles but in the usual middle-European medieval peasant-dress of the traditional story world. In addition, these stories only occur in the later books of the series, to be read by older children.

This analysis and speculative interpretation of the multiple realities of the story world concerns only the meanings of the teachers. No imputations are made of the orientation of the authors, although W. Murray, author of the *Ladybird* series, is described as a lecturer and headmaster, and E.R. Boyce, author of the *Gay Way* series has also written several books on infant education, so that both have the status of 'experts' in this field. Nor is any imputation made about the meanings that children assign to the experiences of reading these stories or of having others read to them. Sometimes it appeared to teachers that some children had not properly defined the story world as a different order of reality. A boy's mother reported he had nightmares after hearing his teacher read the story of Daedelus and Icarus. In telling me about it the teacher said, 'And I did tell them it was only a story'.

Writing - the reproduction of realities

From a study of the children's writing it was clear that they were able to reproduce these story worlds.

> Once upon a time there was a cat and it had five kittens one was called ping, one was pong and the other three were called Dong Wong and Song. One day mother cat took Dong and Wong to the shops and she bought some toys and they lived happily ever after.
>
> Once upon a time there was a princess and she was called Jane and one day she went out to meet her father and a witch peeped round the corner and got her and her mother saw it and Janes father came home and he saw the witch killing her and the king killed the witch and then he got Jane and he toke her home with him and put her in bed and made her better.

The teachers managed the children's writing of news so that they ordered its reality separately from that of a story.

> If it were your story-book you could tell me you've been in a Red Arrow, but you've not actually been in a Red Arrow - this is your newsbook. [N.B. Red Arrows are an aircraft display team.]

News was supposed to relate to the 'real' world and to orthodox reality, similar to that of the 'real' life stories in their reading books.

Creativity and Conventional Reality

Every day, every child did a drawing or painting, which, to begin with, they were allowed to define in their own way. (Teacher, looking at girl's drawing, 'I like it, what is it?')

In the following example the boy had defined painting as covering a surface with paint.

> Teacher introduces the new boy (his second day in school) to painting. He is shown the easel, the paints, the brushes and the apron he must wear, but he is not told how or what to paint. He uses one colour to cover most of the paper. Another boy says to him, 'What are you painting?' He replies, 'A colour'. The other boy, 'A colour, just blue!' He changes brushes and completes the painting in green.

In the absence of the teacher defining a drawing or painting, young children learnt from one another; a whole table frequently did the same basic drawing by copying. The familiar images were those of houses, trees and flowers. These were seen by some teachers as expressions of the children's needs for security and as a therapeutic introduction to school. A few of the younger ones drew on the authority of 'what they told us at college' to support this.

The representations of houses, trees, flowers and

people were versions of cultural images of these things. Although not directly presented to children by the teachers, these were displayed in the classroom, other than in other children's paintings and drawings. Lollypop trees and houses based on a rectangle and a triangle were found on lotto cards, teacher-prepared and commercial word and number cards, mathematics work books and in some story books.

Left to define paintings for themselves the children drew on the limited resources around them but to the teacher their limited images were an indication of the limited resources within them; their relative immaturity. I tried a simple, ethically acceptable, experiment one day. A boy was about to paint. I asked him what he was going to do. 'I don't know.' I suggested, 'Why don't you paint a boat?' The teacher was quite excited when she asked him her usual question, 'Tell me about your picture', and he replied, 'It's a boat'. 'He's never done anything like that before', she said to me later. At least three other children, following his example, 'progressed' to painting boats that day.

These early drawings and paintings were defined by the teachers as expressions of childish innocence. (Teacher, looking at boy's painting, 'Cubist. I suppose he'll lost all that soon').

Children were emancipated from their innocence by the actions of their teachers. After a period in which they could paint or draw what they wished, older children's images were monitored by the teacher's comments so as to introduce more elements of conventional reality. (Teacher, 'Where's the door on your house?'. Girl, 'Hasn't got one'. Teacher, 'How do you get in?').

The conventional reality that the children were required to represent was often more a conventional picture reality.